La Chicana and the Intersection of Race, Class, and Gender

LA CHICANA
AND THE
INTERSECTION
OF
RACE, CLASS,
AND
GENDER

IRENE I. BLEA

New York
Westport, Connecticut
London

1992

Library of Congress Cataloging-in-Publication Data

Blea, Irene I. (Irene Isabel)
La Chicana and the intersection of race, class, and gender / Irene I. Blea
p. cm.
Includes bibliographical references and index.
ISBN 0-275-93980-4 (alk. paper). — ISBN 0-275-93982-0 (pbk : alk. paper)
1. Mexican American women—History. 2. Mexican American women—Social conditions. 3. Feminism—United States. I. Title.
E184.M5B56 1992
305.48'86872073—dc20 90-28075

British Library Cataloguing in Publication Data is available.

Library of Congress Catalog Card Number: 90-28075
ISBN: 0-275-93980-4 (hb.)
0-275-93982-0 (pb.)

First published in 1992

Praeger Publishers, One Madison Avenue, New York, NY 10010
An imprint of Greenwood Publishing Group, Inc.

Printed in the United States of America

The paper used in this book complies with the Permanent Paper Standard issued by the National Information Standards Organization (Z39.48-1984).

10 9 8 7 6 5 4 3 2 1

To Regina
To the women who came before her,
to the women who come with her, and
to the women who will follow

Contents

Preface

The purpose of this work is to outline the academic examination and social reality of La Chicana and to update the social sciences on the intersection of race (or ethnicity), class, and gender. To accomplish this I have included an analysis of the use of language and labels. The study explores the history of Chicanas and examines their socialization, the consequences of deviating from prescribed gender roles, and the emergence of Hispanic women on the national scene in politics, health care, economics, education, religion, and criminal justice. The text also concentrates on the shared lives of Mexican-American women and men at home, in barrios, and elsewhere.

A Chicana is generally thought of as a Mexican-American female, a minority female whose life is characterized by racism and sexism. Rarely do scholars view her within a class context. The Chicana has been perceived as a woman who struggles to overcome the barriers of racism and sexism, but little attention has been given to her power, her cultural productions, her successes and social rewards. This work does so. Chicanas are presented as women who are characterized by a culture rooted in the Spanish language, but who are contemporary women. They are American women of Mexican ancestry.

Generally, the term *Chicana* has feminist connotations, but it may also denote simply feminine gender. Chicanas have been referred to as Spanish, Mexican, Hispanic, Chicano, and Latino females. The word *Chicana* is rooted in the Chicano movement of the 1960s and is a political, ideological term describing a group of people with shared cultural characteristics and shared political interpretations of their experiences. Therefore, some Latinas who are not Mexican-American also refer to themselves as Chicanas. In fact, the term *Chicana*, like *Chicano*, self-selectly identifies women with a certain ideology.

Basically, the term *Chicano* implies an understanding of the history of neglect and discrimination endured by Mexican-American people in the United States. Those who understand this frequently advocate on behalf of their people. Generally, they are called civil rights activists, or members of a grassroots movement. Not all Hispanics or Latinos relate positively to this activism.

The term *Hispanic* refers to persons of Spanish language culture and may include Central Americans and Latin Americans, persons from Cuba and Puerto Rico, Spanish Europeans, and Chicanos. *Latino* also refers to the groups above, but includes Mexico and Central and Latin America. Any persons from this group may call themselves Chicano if they are male, Chicana if they are female.

In this text, the words *Mexican-American, Chicana, Hispanic,* and *Latina* are frequently used. Here an attempt is made to keep the meaning consistent with the definitions above. The reader should be aware that other scholars often use the terms interchangeably.

Chapter 1 of this text reviews the literature on Chicanas and examines their participation in the women's movement, the Chicano movement, and the movement of people of color. It places Chicana scholars within the context of Chicano studies, women's studies, and the social sciences.

The second chapter reviews the conquest of Mexico. It concentrates on the Spanish conquest of the Aztecs, the blending of their two cultures, and the creation of the story of La Llorona as such a cultural blend.

The third chapter reviews the life of Hispanic women in colonial Mexico and in the United States, focusing on an internal colonial model. It notes that little information exists on women of the Mexican-American War period. Emphasis is on how this war contributed to the shaping of the Mexican-American experience in the United States.

Chapter 4 explores how Americanization after the U.S. war with Mexico disempowered La Chicana. Chicano and Chicana stereotypes emerged during this period and today are manifested in jokes based in folklore, traditional custom, and cultural values.

Chapter 5 outlines the contemporary cultural roles of *la mujer* (woman) and their impact of men's roles. It provides a description of Mexican-American women by age and by community activity.

Chapter 6 reviews the lives of older women, who sometimes face age discrimination in addition to racial (ethnic), class, and gender discrimination. These women are also presented as providing stability to the culture.

Chapter 7 discusses how some women have broken old barriers and are defining new roles for La Chicana. This chapter relates how they balance two very strong cultures.

Chapter 8 concentrates on current social issues and compares and contrasts them to the issues of the 1960s. Of outstanding concern are the issues of high school dropouts, teen pregnancy, Chicanas and the Catholic religion, a health incidence report, and Chicanas in prison.

Chapter 9 presents the value of studying racism and ethnicity, class and sexism to gain understanding of how variables intersect, of who hurts and who profits from such a phenomenon. It develops a general theory of discrimination by drawing from the academic work of racial and ethnic minority scholars as well as feminist scholars.

Chapter 10 builds on chapter 9, exploring new directions in the study of Chicanas and examining how the study of La Chicana can lend new direction to the development of feminist theory.

This book is written to advance understanding of the above issues. To some this is perhaps its greatest value. To others this book may assist in breaking through some of the social resistance encountered by minority women. For yet others it might be merely interesting reading. I wrote the book for all these reasons. But mostly I wrote the book in an effort to bring about the end of discrimination.

Chapter 1

Chicana Scholarship and the Third World Perspective

To provide the setting for the study of La Chicana, this chapter reviews the early literature on Chicanas, examining their participation in the women's movement, the Chicano movement, and the movement of people of color in order to illustrate how the analysis of the intersection of race (ethnicity), class, and gender evolved. This analysis is consistent with the Third World perspective also focused upon here.

Chicana scholars are seen within the context of the analysis of structural forces that place them in specific social situations. This chapter reviews the study of La Chicana in Chicano studies, women's studies, and the social sciences, with particular interest in who the Chicana is and where she exists in contemporary scholarship.

FIRST-GENERATION SCHOLARSHIP

Cynthia Orozco brings back painful memories when she writes about the development of Chicana feminism in the Chicano movement and in Chicano studies (Cordova *et al.,* 1986). She reviews the resistance to Chicana feminism and recalls that La Chicana has only recently been studied, beginning in the late 1960s. The review of the first generation of Chicana scholarship quickly focuses on the study of racism and sexism. To combine the two areas is to provide the basis of a general theory of discrimination in this country. Add the dimension of class, and there emerges a multifaceted cycle of discrimination. It is a cycle that must include the many coping mechanisms, human reactions, and creations that allow people to function in society.

Certainly the study of the Chicana brings these phenomena together in a manner advancing research in the social sciences, but this cannot be done unless one considers the historical analysis of La Chicana and her people. This produces an interdisciplinary scholarship that explains her status within both her own and the dominant culture.

Most general discussions on racism and sexism draw attention to the victimization of racial and ethnic minorities and the need to eradicate these forces. There was a time when people thought that to stop racism was the right, moral thing to do. Today, the argument has changed a bit. Racism also needs to end not only because it is morally wrong but also because it would be the economically and politically expedient thing to do. For racism costs—it costs money, time, and resources—and it hampers international relations. Major corporations like U.S. West have discovered that discrimination on the job affects the bottom line: dollars and cents. Marketing firms have discovered that minority populations have a viable middle class, a population with money to spend. Marketing specialists want to tap this relatively new market, and so they also have engaged in the research of La Chicana and her people.

Hispanics alone are estimated to have from 98 to 145 billion dollars to spend on cosmetics, music, beer, and cigarettes. This is why a drive through the barrio will reveal numerous billboards advertising in Spanish. Unfortunately, the products advertised are dangerous to health. Advertising not only on billboards but in magazines and newspapers, on the sides of buses, and on radio and television tends to be for cigarettes and liquor. Aggressive marketing is focused on this new population with relatively new money and with high cigarette and alcohol consumption. Tobacco use (*Hispanic Link Weekly Report*, 1989) and other life-threatening activities like alcohol abuse are high among Chicanos. Depending on country of origin, Hispanic women have increased or held steady their cigarette smoking since its height in the 1950s (*Hispania*, 1989). It remained steady through the 1970s. More Puerto Rican women smoked in 1983 than did Mexican-American or Cuban women. Smoking has declined markedly among Mexican-American men and slightly among Cuban-American and Puerto Rican men (*Hispania*, 1989). Although cigarettes can be dangerous, for smoking increases the risk of cancer, some Chicanos note that such advertising has its merits: At least these major industries are paying attention to the 12 to 20 million Chicanos and Chicanas in the nation.

In addition to economics, there has emerged another reason for doing away with discrimination: the inability of Americans to maintain a leading role in international relations. This failing affects international politics as well as economics. In a sense the world has gotten smaller. Because of technology Americans can communicate easily and rapidly with most people around the globe. They can travel to the other side of the world in a few hours. Yet most Americans lack the skills required for such communication in today's world, since most are monolingual. Americans also tend to be monocultural: Most know how to function in only one culture, their own, and they remain thus at a time in history when cultural literacy is a necessity for a country that has led in many, many fields but now finds itself floundering.

It is in this arena that Chicanos and Chicanas have the advantage and can teach Americans. Thus far, the United States has been unwilling to learn about knowing and functioning in more than one culture, in more than one language. In fact, it has treated people of other cultures, even within its own border, with hostility and aggression. Nevertheless, Chicano bilingual and bicultural abilities have proven worthy in courtrooms, in business transactions, and in international relations.

La Chicana has participated in all these areas, but an interested reader would find little to document that this is so. A study of the Chicana experience, however, quickly lends insight into Chicano culture, the dominant society, and the structural forces that affect the Chicano quality of life.

Very early research on La Chicana tended to center on her as a cultural person. Culture is seen, for the most part, as the variable influencing Chicana participation in folklore, marriage, health and healing, education, mothering, and political activism. Maxine Baca-Zinn (1982) pointed this out when she reviewed three early works: Evangelina Enriquez and Alfredo Mirande's *La Chicana: The Mexican-American Woman* (1979), Margarita Melville's *Twice a Minority: Mexican-American Women* (1980), and Magdelina Mora and Adelaida Del Castillo's *Mexican Women in the United States: Struggles Past and Present* (1980). Her work and other first-generation scholarship spent much energy revising the work of past scholars, but they also produced material where traditionally there was none and inaugurated discussions on the impact of structural forces that locate women within specific social strata in society. In this process the first generation of scholars also documented the consequences of deviating from prescribed social roles.

Baca-Zinn and other Chicana feminist scholars further the propensity to include the analysis of social control in discussions on race (ethnicity), class, and gender. Basically, the thought is that race (a genetic variable) and/or ethnicity (a cultural and social variable) plus gender (another genetic variable) and class (also a cultural or social variable) interact with one another in a complex of patterns that render La Chicana disadvantaged, or at least perceived to be disadvantaged, as she functions in a contemporary world.

The examination of La Chicana has not been without its problems. Information has been unavailable, inconsistent, and erroneous. This should not be interpreted to mean that scholars are not attempting to standardize data or are not conscientiously writing about La Chicana. They are. Many are graduate and undergraduate students, some are professors, and a few are men who write about her. Mostly, however, these are women and researchers with very limited vehicles for publication and dissemination of their material.

Many Hispanic women are currently attempting to address these difficulties by producing newsletters and monographs. However, these publications are sporadic and difficult to locate in most libraries. Until recently, it was even difficult to know how many Chicanas there were in the United States. This problem has been corrected by redefinition and reorganization of data-collecting techniques.

CHICANA SCHOLARSHIP AND THE CHICANO MOVEMENT

Chicanas have taken on the responsibility for documenting their story by giving direction to demographic surveys, engaging in various academic pursuits, and promoting Chicana feminist scholarship. Most Chicana feminist scholarship has been interdisciplinary, combining information from various disciplines to document the Chicana experience holistically.

Indeed, minority women tend to have a more holistic view of the world because they recognize their lives have been shaped by a number of factors that do not affect other women. They experience many social pressures and stresses at one time. They tend to draw from a variety of experiences in order to learn and teach and communicate. They also have special knowledge because their experience has been different, even unique, since being female is complicated by being a minority, which is further complicated by the unequal distribution of resources and class.

Often the way in which minority women say and do things is thought of as unusual, strange, even wrong. But women, especially minority women, have experienced a unique way of coping with life's circumstances, which include Anglo men and women. Coping mechanisms, discussed elsewhere in the book, are an area in need of additional research, one that leads to new and exciting academic developments.

When Chicanas began doing research, they generally started by recording Chicano history that had been transmitted orally from one generation to another. They wrote about their personal experiences as well as the experiences of their people. Some early writers include Anna Nieto Gomez, Marcella Lucero Trujillo, Irene I. Blea, Ines Hernandez Tovar, Inés Talamantez, and Lea Ybarra. These women were also heavily involved in higher education and in the Chicano movement of the 1960s, an involvement that influenced their scholarship and led some of them to create literary as well as academic work.

A prime example of such work was that of Marcella Lucero Trujillo. Lucero Trujillo was born in Alamosa, Colorado, and died in Denver, where she had been a member of Rodolfo "Corky" Gonzales's Crusade for Justice. She and many other women and men worked on a variety of Chicano issues. Lucero Trujillo was active not only in the Southwest but also in the Midwest, where she studied and addressed issues of education, housing, and youth. Her most memorable work combined prison reform, poetry, and the development of Chicano studies. Lucero Trujillo's poems frequently combined elements of her analytical work and her activism with descriptions of the environment. She was among the first to publish feminist poetry. Other early feminist poets who also wrote about the environment include Ines Hernandez Tovar (who later wrote under the name Ines Hernandez), Ines Talamantes, Carmen Tafolla, and Irene I. Blea. In their poetry Chicanas frequently related how they became motivated to struggle against racism and sexism.

A full Chicana feminist perspective emerged in the late 1960s and early 1970s. The scholarship was consistent with ideological developments in the Chicano movement and the Chicano community. The women named above and others like them completed their education, earning master's and doctorate degrees. All of them eventually taught on university and college campuses, and all of them advocated women's rights both within the women's movement and the Chicano movement. They did this, however, with much resistance.

CHICANA SCHOLARSHIP AND THE FEMINIST MOVEMENT

At the height of social criticism in the United States, Anglo feminist issues were very much at the forefront. Chicanas related well to these concerns, as they experienced sexism within their own movement, their own families, and their communities. Some early feminist interests included female-male relationships, equal pay for equal work, and the right of women to control their own bodies through access to birth control and abortion. Poverty was a concern, but it was nowhere near the top of the list. Foremost among feminist issues for La Chicana was poverty. Her people were poor. The women listed above came from poor backgrounds or were from first-generation working-class families. All feminists wanted to be represented in higher levels of employment, education, politics, and decision making. Chicanas especially wanted this on behalf of their people, since they ranked even lower than Anglo women in all aspects of society.

Chicanas and other minority women struggled to take part in the feminist movement, but the movement was middle class and Anglo controlled. Indeed, the early feminist movement of the 1960s was unsuccessful in addressing issues of particular relevance to Chicanas and other minority females (Pesquera and Segura, 1989). Women of color withdrew into their own feminist movement within their own racial or ethnic groups and simultaneously proceeded with the civil rights movement.

Most Chicanas, like most black women, never abandoned their men and their people while striving to gain equal rights for women. As black and Chicano women talked and worked with one another, they discovered they were having the same experiences with the Anglo feminist movement and civil rights movement. Black women were reacting much the same as Chicanas. They, too, remained loyal to the black civil rights movement even as they addressed feminist concerns within that movement. At this time they began to be referred to as minority women.

These "minority" women would form coalitions at meetings and conferences. In fact, they were among the first coalition builders of the U.S. civil rights movement. By forming coalitions they developed an ideology that strengthened the movement. This ideology has yet to be recognized.

Anglo women wanted women of color to do the impossible: to choose between being female and being a person of color. However, the women of color would not and could not choose. They proceeded to address their own concerns and the concerns of their own people while they presented an analysis of the intersection of race (ethnicity), class, and gender. This analysis took place in various communities and on campuses, but neither the Anglo-feminist nor the civil rights movement paid much attention. The struggle to get these movements to hear and understand this argument was, to say the least, intense. It contributed to the fragmentation of the women's movement.

Until the late 1970s the Anglo-dominated feminist movement remained fragmented on the issues of racism, socialism, class, and lesbian women.With the exception of racism, much of this has been resolved. When Chicanas were involved, they tended to sympathize with the socialist women who advocated the overthrow of capitalism and the construction of an entirely different social structure; but they did not join in any great numbers the Communist or Socialist Worker party, the stronghold of this perspective. Lesbianism was too far removed from the reality of the predominantly Catholic women, and experience has shown that the concern of ethnicity consumes issues of sexual preference. Homophobia still exists among some feminists because heterosexuality is the ideal in American society. Being white Anglo-American is also espoused as the social ideal. However, lesbianism and the civil rights of lesbian women are no longer issues as divisive as they once were. Racism, on the other hand, is frequently reported, and Chicanas do not flock to join NOW or any other national, Anglo-dominated feminist organization.

In the social sciences these issues were of some concern, but Anglo women concentrated efforts on creating women's studies, while Chicano females and males concentrated on creating Chicano studies. These critical thinkers had concluded that their side of the American story had not been told, and they would have to tell it themselves. The separate studies revolved around the repression of women and the repression of people of color. There was little discussion between the two factions. Each designed a curriculum that centered upon stereotypes, the use of language, and perceived social, psychological, and biological differences. Women's studies analyzed gender roles and women and work, women and the law, the history of women, women and the capitalist system, sexual harassment, the struggle for liberation, lesbianism, childcare, violence, mother-daughter relationships, friends, and, finally, Third World women. Chicanos analyzed race roles, race and ethnic caste, minorities and the law, the history of minorities, minorities and the capitalist system, racial violence, the struggle for liberation, mistreatment and misrepresentation in education, and various local and regional community issues.

La Chicana wanted to be included among the topics of discussion, but she had to force the issue and develop her own class, La Chicana. Thus the first courses were offered in Chicano studies. Today La Chicana still grapples to get her voice heard in both women's studies and Chicano studies (Baca-Zinn et al., 1986).

CHICANAS AND THIRD WORLD WOMEN

Anglo and Chicana attention to La Chicana and other minority women has come to be broadly discussed under the liberal label of Third World women and has been enveloped within the internal colonial model, in part because the combined issues of class, race, and gender are rooted in U.S. colonialization of Mexico's northern territory. The model is historical; it explains the violence of war and its resulting subjugation of a people and calls for liberation. Consistent with Third World issues, the concerns about class, race, and gender are much the same as they were several years ago. If there has been social change, it has been minimal.

Concentration upon the Chicana as a Third World woman was and is based upon the idea that two countries control the world: the United States and the Soviet Union. The political sphere of which the United States is the center is commonly referred to as the West, while that centering on the Soviet Union is the East. Unaffiliated or underdeveloped countries are referred to as the Third World. This view very skillfully places countries other than the United States and the Soviet Union in a secondary and subordinate position. Feminists adopted the idea of the Third World from an Anglo, male-dominated language and incorporated it into their own language and scholarship to refer to those women most disenfranchised from the dominant power structure: women of black, Hispanic, Asian, and Native American origin. These minority women are also citizens of the United States and therefore, let it not be forgotten, are the political sisters of feminists.

Chicanas have not criticized the Third World perspective. Indeed, they understand the relationship of the powerful and the powerless. However, they have not noted that to be classified as Third World deprives them of American status in America. Black, Hispanic, Asian, and Native American women should be called what they are. To engage in classification further alienates American women of color from Anglo women and plays into the male-dominated orientation toward power and the debasement of the powerless. Other alienating experiences include not being recognized by Anglo feminists as having a feminist perspective, resistance to lending legitimacy to Chicana scholarship, and the inability of Anglo women to share power with women of color.

This debased position, plus the early feminist experiences of American women of color, has been extremely harmful, and few minority women have forgotten the past, or forgiven it. In contrast, few Anglo women have even acknowledged these experiences. They have made no apology, no effort to redress wrongs, nor any attempt to understand, for they remain part of the dominant cultural sphere. Institutionalized racism, sexism, and classism have thus created a division between feminists of color and other feminists.

White women had a history of addressing women's issues in the United

States, Chicanas did not. Their feminist history was in Mexico. In the United States they had a history of addressing racism. Many Anglo feminists perceived Chicana hesitancy to embrace their movement as a lack of feminist experience and commitment. This, of course, was not true. Whereas Chicanas wanted a change in the system, Anglo women simply wanted power within the existing structure.

RESISTANCE FROM WITHIN

For striving toward a different society, Chicanas were frequently thought of as deviant. Women who have wanted to change traditional gender roles, the socialization process, and gender-typed opportunities for women are often thought of as deviant; they are not normal, but somehow strange. Generally, social deviance is measured by the degree to which individuals differ from those who conform to the norm. For Chicanas there are four norms: An Anglo norm, a Chicano norm, and norms for women in both of these groups. Frequently, the norms are not always the same. The trick, then, is for the Chicana to select a balanced lifestyle for herself, for if she strays from cultural prescriptions, there is always a negative consequence.

The degree to which behavior is defined as deviant depends on what kind of violations take place. A particular behavior may seem only eccentric in one situation but deviant in another. Generally both cultures recognize deviance when strong cultural norms are violated. Thus, few acts are intrinsically deviant, and it can be said that deviance is culturally relevant.

Usually the powerful impose upon the less powerful definitions of what is deviant. In the case of the Chicana, for example, Anglo society and Chicano men have defined what is an appropriate role for her. Usually the study of deviance has two concerns: One focuses upon who is doing the defining; the other, upon who is being defined. To understand the life of La Chicana, that life must be viewed from within the Chicana experience. The Chicana experience is circumscribed by formal and informal sanctions. At a formal level are spoken and written rules; but there are informal rules, also monitored, that exist as unspoken rules in the society. There exists a cultural norm—a rule establishing what is culturally acceptable. Outside this area social behavior becomes distasteful, hardly tolerable, and even unacceptable. The more one deviates from the norm, the less the behavior is valued or tolerated. There are statistical models that reflect standard deviations from the norm, that is, the degree to which people or groups deviate from what is defined as normal. Generally, the further one deviates from the norm, the smaller the number of people represented and the higher the deviance. (See bell curve.)

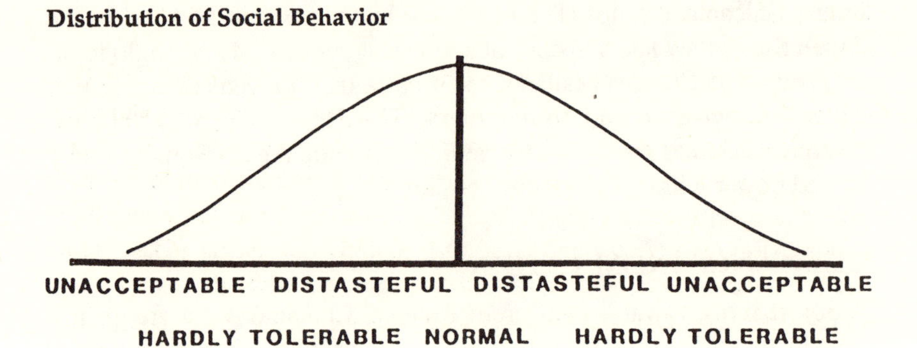

Perhaps the most frequently cited explanation for what causes deviance is Emile Durkheim's concept of anomie. As society grows and changes, the norms become more unclear and people are more diverse. The old norms are no longer applicable; and because people cannot function without norms, they may even commit suicide (1897; 1966). Robert Merton asserted that some individuals do not find the norms relevant to them (1957). This increases their potential for deviance. Merton's model stopped focusing on the individual and paid attention to the social structure and how it bans some individuals from attaining the means by which they can be "normal."

Such is the Chicano condition. Given most dominant values and norms in the United States, Chicanos cannot be "normal" in American society only because they are not Anglo. Anglo racial prejudice and the fact that Chicano culture is too different from Anglo culture prevent Chicanos from fitting the norm. Some Chicanos have found a comfortable blend of norms. Others select what is the most comfortable and diminish the impact of the other culture as much as possible. Even when some Chicanos attain higher education, upward mobility, and other symbols of American success, generally, the dominant social system will not tolerate too many Chicanos near the white Anglo standard of material, physical, and emotional stability. Thus, from a sociological perspective, it makes sense for the Chicano to be viewed as abnormal within the context of Anglo-dominated American society. Conversely, one can note that Anglos frequently appear normal from the Chicano perspective.

Anglo society is more interested in keeping the Chicano abnormal than the Chicano is in doing the same to the Anglo. Chicano resistance threatens Anglo dominance, and this is why Anglo society places pressure on the Chicano to be more like Anglos. Thus Chicanos and Chicanas are often told they must change their ways, and increase their cultural adherence.

White America does not want Chicanos in power. Anglos fear Chicanos will treat them the ways Anglos have treated Chicanos and other minorities. Anglo America also does not want its people to know that it sets up people of color to be anomic deviants. It sets them up to accept or strive to meet society's goals, but it blocks them from achieving those goals. Anglo America wants and needs to deny this aspect of its character in order to continue feeling superior at a time when its superiority is being denied by growing numbers of people all over the world.

Another theory frequently used to understand deviance is that of cultural transmission. Most representative of this perspective is Edwin Sutherland's (1961) differential association theory, which assumes that deviance is learned through interaction with others. In cultural transmission theories, deviant norms and values are transmitted as cultural characteristics. Sutherland's work is harmful, especially because it has set the tone of research and theory for more than thirty years. It fails to recognize the social factors that contribute to a definition of deviance that victimize people of color. Fortunately, this kind of thinking is wavering.

A theory that does look at some social factors in the creation of deviance is social-control theory (Hirschi, 1969; Krohn and Massey, 1980; Nye, 1958; Reckless, 1973; Wiatrowski, Griswold, and Roberts, 1981). For these theorists deviance is a natural condition, and it is its absence that needs focus. Travis Hirschi (1969) suggests deviance is absent when people are not strongly bonded to society. When people are strongly bonded, then society is exerting powerful, informal, social control. When they are weakly bonded, informal control is weak.

When Chicanas and other women step outside socially prescribed roles, they are addressing their alienation from society's norm. They are attempting to take control of their own lives. When this is not happening, it should not be assumed that everything is right. In fact, their failure to step outside socially prescribed roles may mean Chicanas are being repressed; they might have accepted a lifestyle defined by someone else and feel powerless to change it.

Chicano scholars (Blea, 1988; Mirande, 1985; Barrera, 1979; Acuna, 1981) have documented the double standards, formal and informal, that exist for Chicanos. For example, at the formal (manifest) level Chicanos are equal under the law. At the informal level there are special ways of interpreting the laws that apply to people of color, thereby creating a double standard and producing weak social bonding to the dominant norm. Women have experienced this; it is therefore not surprising that they do not easily trust male-dominated systems.

Anglo (especially Anglo male) deviance is normal to Chicanos and Chicanas. Many Chicanos are persons of honor who traditionally have been cooperative and trusting with another. When they are not, it is because they have had negative experiences with the dominant systems.

Because Chicanos have not accepted all Anglo norms and values, and because they have their own norms and values, they are not as strongly controlled by dominant society in the informal way that Anglos are controlled by their own society. Negative consequences are a result of their constant struggle for power and social control.

The Chicana, of course, has endured negative social consequences for resisting control in both societies. Some women remain angry women. Some have given up, while others have come to believe that to struggle against sexist oppression is not their concern. Still others are too oppressed to recognize they are oppressed.

The Chicano is very much aware of the double standard: a dual wage system, dual social standards, and dual opportunities. Chicanas are aware that this system is even more finely stratified where they are concerned. They recognize a multilevel standard of justice, education, and value judgment of cultural productions like literature and art. Noting that there are more blacks and Chicanas in criminal cases and as prisoners than there are Anglo women, they recognize the negative attitudes and behaviors directed at them. They recognize that too few Chicanas act as representatives of that system. They know police officers have killed and brutally beaten Chicano men and women and children. When the United States propagates the myth of peaceful progress, Chicanas recognize the lies and distortions. This is why Chicana feminists cannot and will not abandon Chicano issues for solely feminist issues.

SOME CHOOSE TO BE FEMINISTS

Chicanas and other women of color have faced feminist issues from a different focus. Chicana feminists made extremely difficult decisions, often against the resistance of mothers, friends, fathers, brothers, other women, and men. For example, Anglo women strongly protested that most people preferred their firstborn to be male. This attitude put women in second place. Although this view permeated their experience, generally the gender of their firstborn did not matter to Chicanas. Their concern was that their baby be healthy. Their high regard for health and human life negated the issue. Unfortunately, Anglo women perceived their attitude as lack of understanding of what it meant to be a feminist.

Chicanas experienced resistance from their men and other Chicanas. Chicano men initially teased and then became angry. Later a few of them joined the Chicanas in their feminist argument, but they laughed and called the women *comadres*. Used thus, in a demeaning, derogatory way, the term implied that the women had nothing better to do than "gossip" or "bitch." *Comadre*, however, has its root in the socially defined kin and nonkin relationships of Spanish-origin women. Unknowingly, the men who teased and criticized by using this term undermined their own efforts and encouraged the sisterhood that Chicanas shared.

There were Chicanas who also resisted Chicana feminists and who tended to agree with the men. They felt the movement was unnecessary, that it fragmented the Chicano movement and disrupted family and culture, and that Chicanas had "sold out" by wanting what white women wanted. For the most part, these women were older, religious, and either unaccustomed to or afraid of self-determination.

Men not only criticized women for drawing attention and energy away from the Chicano movement and into a movement having little to do with Chicanas; they also criticized Chicanas for destroying the basis of Chicano culture: the family. During the highly controversial *Roe v. Wade* arguments, many Chicanos viewed abortion and birth control as forms of genocide. Chicano males charged that birth control and abortion were a white attempt at cultural and physical genocide, an elimination of the ethnic group. They espoused that some Anglos felt that if fewer Chicanos were born, Anglos could maintain better control.

Chicanas wanted and needed control of their own bodies in order to control the quality of their lives. They did not want men dictating in this sphere. Too many children resulted in poor health and poverty, but forced sterilization was also an issue. Anglo doctors and other officials were forcing women of color to become sterilized. Often women consented to sterilization while under sedation, or they were coerced into signing consent forms in order not to lose social security and welfare benefits.

Chicana feminists persisted in drawing attention to minority female concerns and noted that sexism, like racism, functioned to the disadvantage of all women in a class society. Historically these were loud, angry, and hostile times, times of Vietnam War protests, boycotts of grape and lettuce purchases, demonstrations on college campuses, sit-ins, and pickets. Hippies were singing love and peace songs and wearing flowers in their hair. White youth, women, Asians, Native Americans, blacks, and Chicanos and Chicanas were all active at the same time.

During this critical and crucial era Chicanas and Chicanos were walking out of public schools in protest of a curriculum that excluded their story, and in protest of culturally biased and unjust academic standards. Men and women in the United States changed from wearing traditional clothing with strong gender-typed fashion to more casual and androgenous attire. Jeans and T-shirts were donned as the latest fashion; before, they had been the attire of the working class. Drugs were plentiful; and poverty, simplicity, and rebellion were common. The nation was ablaze with activity. At no other time were young women and young men more active and visible on the streets, in schools, in the media, in the parks, everywhere.

During this time Chicanas were adamant about the need to eliminate racism and sexism. Anglo feminists pointed out that Mexican men were the biggest sexists of all. Chicana feminists agreed that some were sexist, but also believed that generally this stereotype of Chicano men was itself both racist and sexist. When Anglo feminists responded with their ultimatum–choose between being female and being Chicano—Chicanas tried to explain that they could not and would not choose, for they were poor physically, culturally, and socially, and Chicano and female at the same time.

In the 1960s Lyndon B. Johnson made poverty a campaign issue in his War on Poverty, making federal money available to address a variety of social issues. At the same time society changed. Men and women grew their hair long. Some women no longer shaved their underarms and legs. Free love and sex without guilt were the order of the day. Chicanas and other women of color joined in. They were few, but they effectively drew attention to their own issues. They never deserted their people, and they never deserted the Chicano movement.

Instead, they took inspiration from their history. They continued to develop the Chicano experience by becoming knowledgeable about thei-history and the contributions of Chicanas. They knew that as the American West developed, Chicanos became increasingly displaced from the land, especially after 1848 and the end of the Mexican-American War. They learned about Francisca Reyes Esparza, and they followed her example in leading their struggle. Esparza addressed the issue of land displacement. While attempting to gather evidence to file a land grant lawsuit for titles to a quarter of a million acres of oil and ranch land, Esparza was successful in developing communication between the United States and Mexico. She became an expert on the historical aspects of old land titles guaranteed to Mexican-American citizens under Article VIII of the

Treaty of Guadelupe Hidalgo. In 1946 she won her landright case and set in motion vehicles utilized today on those same issues. Esparza's contributions are overshadowed by those of Burt Corona, praised by today's Chicano leaders and academics for the labor causes he rightfully pursued.

Another Chicana overshadowed by Corona is Josefina Fierro, who became active during the mass deportations of the 1930s. Fierro was involved in bringing Mexican-American citizens back from Mexico. In the early 1940s she joined Corona in organizing low-paid Hispanic workers employed in canneries and on farms. Fierro was further instrumental in ending the violent racist and sexist conflicts between Chicano citizens and U.S. servicemen after World War II in Los Angeles. By negotiating with Vice-President Wallace to declare Los Angeles out of bounds to military personnel, Fierro became the most important person in the termination of the Zoot Suit conflicts. Many Chicano history books make these Zoot riots appear to be solely racist in nature, but the truth is that they were also sexist. Chicanas were the victims of U.S. servicemen who considered them to be cheap prostitutes and/or infected with venereal disease and addicted to marijuana. Women were being slandered and harassed by servicemen. Interviews with ex-Zoot Suit defendants reveal that Chicanos were also sexist in their attitudes toward Chicanas: The Hispanic men did not want to share their women with the "gringo." Much fighting took place, and today the Chicana still suffers from such racist-sexist stereotypes.

This text would not be complete without mention of Chicana activists in the labor market, but it should not proceed without mentioning that U.S. labor history is a most violent history characterized by killings and beatings. Some of this activity gained national headlines, but some of it is little known, like the 1913 Christmas riot in Los Angeles. On a rainy Christmas day 500 Chicano women and men gathered to protest economic conditions. They were brutally disrupted, injured, and arrested (Escobar, 1988). This activity, like other worker-organized activity all over the country, is best understood within the context of labor relations in the country at the time. The struggle was basically between the owners of the means of production and the workers. Owners sought to keep profit margins high. Workers strove for a higher wage and to gain negotiating power by organizing into unions. Some unions were hesitant to allow Chicanos as members, but Chicanos and Chicanas did join unions and to this day remain very active in the labor movement.

Emma Tenayuca and Delores Huerta are but two of a large number of women active in labor organizing. The list also includes Lucy

Parsons and Louisa Moreno as well as numerous contemporary women—faceless and nameless individuals working to gain job security, healthy working conditions, equal pay, and benefits for workers. Perhaps best remembered for her participation in the San Antonio, Texas, pecan-shelling strike in 1938, Tenayuca was the principal organizer and spokesperson representing primarily Chicana workers, who were protesting wages and work conditions. The strike was extremely successful but lost significance when the processing plants were mechanized and the workers displaced. Worker displacement remains a labor issue, and Tenayuca still engages in dialogue over such issues. Indeed, struggle against oppressive forces has been a lifestyle for many Chicanas.

Women have been instrumental in protecting workers' rights and have organized in fields, factories, communities, and industrial plants across the land. Many of these women have taken part in major efforts such as the Farah Slack strike and boycott, which began on May 9, 1972. During this effort 4,000 Chicano workers, mostly women, walked off their jobs.

Feminist Chicanas have marched and protested the killing of their people by police and have criticized sexist and racist education, repressive religion, and violent rape and attacks on women. Building on a history of creativity, these women continue to struggle and create against oppressing forces in their own culture and in society at large. Their creativity is extended into the social sciences, where Chicana feminist scholars have emerged to examine earlier work. Early feminists are not offended by this examination, for they are well aware that they are engaged in a battle of ideas, and that ideas must be able to withstand criticism or change. At the forefront of early feminist scholarship were women like Marcella Trujillo, Inés Hernandez Tovar, Martha Cotera, Inés Talamantez, Lea Ybarra, Maxine Baca-Zinn, Anna Nieto Gomez, and Irene I. Blea.

Courses and publications on La Chicana were first prepared in the 1970s and cross-listed almost as an afterthought in women's studies. Even today, there is not a regular, tenured-faculty Hispanic female chairperson of a women's studies department on any major campus in the nation; but contemporary Chicana feminist writings can be encountered in a variety of forms: in newsletters, in magazines and periodicals, and even in some academic journals. However, their occurrence is sporadic and therefore difficult to locate in any concentrated academic form.

A review of such literature will reveal that Chicana issues are much the same as they were twenty years ago. Women still earn less money than men. They still encounter resistance from Anglo women. Birth control and abortion are still major concerns, and the Chicano community is still divided on abortion.

In 1972 the Chicana Caucus met at the National Chicano Political Conference in San Jose, California. The conference adopted a lengthy position paper on the concerns of Chicanas, focusing on jobs, child care, education, and abortion. At the first National Convention of La Raza Unida party in September, 1972, the party pledged support of Chicana issues (La Raza Unida Archives, 1987). At these meetings, as well as at the National Association of Chicano Studies meetings, there was resistance to abortion, but in the long run Chicanas discovered that politically sophisticated men were not as sexist as most of the nation would like to believe.

Nevertheless, Christine Sierra (Cordova et al., 1988) documents that on the question of legalized abortion there has been some Chicano agreement with the Reagan administration's position on the subject. Sierra draws from Rodolfo O. De la Garza and Robert R. Brischetto (1983) to note that 47 percent of Chicanos surveyed during this administration supported legalized abortion under certain circumstances, while 34 percent opposed abortion under any circumstances. It was interesting to note that in 1989, when the right to abortion was a national concern, few Chicanas engaged in pro- or antiabortion activism.

Other issues remain. Chicanas still seek greater representation in education and politics, and they want higher levels of employment. Although some gains were made in the 1960s and 1970s, then lost in the 1980s, long-term goals are far from being reached; support organizations, advocacy groups, and pressure tactics exist as testimonials to this fact.

The Chicano movement was predominantly a nonviolent civil rights movement. Contrary to popular belief, the movement has not ceased; it has, rather, taken on different manifestations (these manifestations will be discussed in future chapters). However, violence against Chicanos who addressed Chicano concerns remains an issue. Chicanas do not escape violence. American Friends worker and guest columnist for the *Hispanic Link Weekly Report* Aurora Camacho de Schmidt writes that nonviolence as a political tool is often resisted, but that passivity among Chicanos is never resisted by the dominant society (1988). Ironically, she notes that nonviolence is only for the very strong. Social, psychological, and spiritual strength has kept Chicanos advocating civil rights.

Academic Chicanas note that academic commitment is a form of this involvement. Chicanas have advanced their scholarship to locate the cause of women's oppression in the combined elements of culture, the structure and function of class, and race and gender in an advanced capitalist society. They perceive capitalism and male dominance in the capitalist structure as contributing to the control of women. Both men and the capitalist structure benefit from women's oppression. Several maintain that only when Chicanas are freed from this condition will all Chicanos be lifted from the grip of oppression.

Many Chicana scholars present papers at academic conferences. Usually there are but a very few at any given conference, except for those conferences whose focus is to bring together Chicanos and Chicanas to discuss academic concerns. One such conference is the National Association of Chicano Studies (NACS). In 1978, NACS elected Irene I. Blea as its first female national chairperson, but the issues of sexism had been addressed by the conference since 1976.

From NACS there have emerged two leading works on la Chicana. *Chicana Voices: Intersections of Class, Race, and Gender* (1986) is a summary of conference proceedings and includes papers on *la mujer* (woman). As a result of work done by women at this and other conferences, Mujeres Activas en Letras y Cambio Social (MALCS) was formed. The organization has produced *Trabajos Monográficos: Studies in Chicana/Latina Research,* a monograph series featuring the academic and literary work of Chicanas. The women of NACS have also formed a Chicana caucus. The primary role of the caucus is to monitor the participation of women in the association. The caucus also supports women and their scholarship by providing a supportive network consisting of other women in the field. A close relationship exists between the NACS caucus and MALCS.

Hard-fought political battles sometimes get forgotten by the younger generation, but the truth is that some Chicanas choose to be feminists. Some early Chicana feminists have died, some have become less active, and some continue with energy to pass on the legacy to the second generation. Positions of privilege are difficult to give up, and many men still resist feminism. However, most Chicano males realize they need and value women. Their culture traditionally teaches them this, although as they become more Americanized, they lose the meaning of the value of women. Chicana and Chicano male activists have contributed much to understanding the multifaceted cycle of discrimination. Today the struggles persist.

REFERENCES

Acuna, Rodolfo. 1981. *Occupied America: A History of Chicanos* (3rd ed.). New York: Harper & Row.

Baca-Zinn, Maxine, Lynn Cannon, Elizabeth Higgenbotham, and Bonnie Thorton Dill. 1986. "The Costs of Exclusionary Practices in Women's Studies." *Signs: Journal of Women in Culture and Society*, Vol. 2, No. 21: 290-303.

Barrera, Mario. 1979. *Race and Class in the Southwest.* South Bend, Ind.: Notre Dame University Press.

Blea, Irene I. 1988. *Toward a Chicano Social Science.* New York: Praeger.

Camacho de Schmidt, Aurora. 1988. "Violence and a Non-Violent Movement." *Hispanic Link Weekly Report*, Vol. 6, No. 44 (November 7): 44.

De la Garza, R., and R. Brischetto. 1983. "The Mexican-American Electorate: Information Sources and Policy Orientations." Occasional Paper No. 2, San Antonio, Texas, Southwest Voter Registration Education Project and the Hispanic Population Studies Program of the Center for Mexican-American Studies. Austin: University of Texas.

Durkheim, Emile. 1966. *Suicide.* Trans. J. Spaulding and George Simpson. New York: Free Press, 1966; original work published 1897.

Escobar, Edward J. 1988. "The Los Angeles Police Department and Mexican Workers: The Case of the 1913 Christmas Riot." In Juan R. Garcia, Julia Curry Rodriguez, and Clara Lomas, eds., *In Times of Challenge: Chicanos and Chicanas in American Society.* 1988. Houston: University of Houston Press, Mexican-American Studies Program, Monograph Series No. 6.

Garcia, Juan R., Julia Curry Rodriguez, and Clara Lomas, eds. 1988. *In Times of Challenge: Chicanos and Chicanas in American Society*. Houston: University of Houston Press, Mexican-American Studies Program, Monograph Series No. 6.

Hirschi, Travis. 1969. *Causes of Delinquency.* Berkeley: University of California Press.

Hispania. 1989. "Hispana Smokers Increase While Men Light Up Less." *Hispania*, Vol. 3, No. 4: 8.

Hispanic Link Weekly Report. 1989. Vol. 7, No. 7 (February 13): 1.

Krohn, Marvin D., and James L. Massey. 1980. "Social Control and Delinquent Behavior: An Examination of the Social Bond." *Sociological Quarterly* 21 (Autumn): 529-43.

Krohn, Marvin, Ronald Akens, Marcia Radosevich, and John Lanza-Kaduce. 1980. "Social Status and Deviance." *Criminology* 18: 303-18.

Melville, Margaritta B. 1980. *Twice a Minority: Mexican American Women.* St. Louis: Mosby Press.

Merton, Robert K. 1957. *Social Theory and Social Structure.* New York: Free Press. 185-248.

Mirande, Alfredo. 1985. *The Chicano Experience*. South Bend, Ind.: University of Notre Dame Press.

Nye, Ivan. 1958. *Family Relationships and Delinquent Behavior.* New York: Wiley.

Orozco, Cynthia. 1986. "Sexism in Chicano Studies and in the Community." In Teresa Cordova et al., eds., *Chicana Voices: Intersections of Class, Race, and Gender*. Austin: CMAS Publications, University of Texas Press. 11-18.

Pesquera, Beatriz M., and Denise Segura. 1989. Paper presented at the Western Social Science Association Annual Conference, Albuquerque, New Mexico. Also appeared as a short synopsis in the 1988 MALCS newsletter.

(La) Raza Unida Archives. 1972/1987. Position paper, untitled. In 1987, the University of Texas, Benson Latin-American Collection, housed a number of pamphlets, minutes, position papers, agendas, and other documentation relevant to La Raza Unida.

Reckless, Walter C. 1973. *The Crime Problem* (5th ed.). New York: Appleton-Century-Crofts.

Sierra, Christine M. 1988. "Chicano Politics after 1984." In Juan R. Garcia, Julia Curry Rodriguez, and Clara Lomas, eds., *In Times of Challenge: Chicanos and Chicanas in American Society*. Houston: University of Houston Press, Mexican-American Studies Program, Monograph Series No. 6: 7-24.

Sutherland, Edwin H. 1961. *White Collar Crime.* New York: Holt, Rinehart and Winston.

U.S. Department of Commerce, Bureau of the Census. *Statistical Abstract of the United States*, 108th Ed., December, 1987. Washington, D.C.: GPO.

Wiatrowski, Michael D., David B. Griswold, and Mary K. Roberts. 1981. "Social Control Theory and Delinquency." *American Sociological Review* 46 (October): 525-41.

Chapter 2

Spanish Impact on the Changing Roles of New World Women

This chapter analyzes what Chicanas inherit from the clash and the blending of Spanish and Indian cultures. It surveys the indigenous experience of women before the arrival of the Spanish. The story of La Llorona is presented as a cultural blend of indigenous and European roots. This chapter draws attention to the story of La Llorona, its meaning and its moral and messages about the nature of the women born of two cultures.

MESO-AMERICA AND THE PRE-COLUMBIAN PERIOD

Chicano scholars in the United States began their study early. However, in the 1960s they seriously concentrated on Mexico, the effect of European influences, and their roots in the American Southwest. Initially, however, academics and those involved in the Chicano movement concentrated their study upon the Aztecs in the central valley of Mexico. They also focused attention upon the Mayans in the southern part of Mexico. Scholars refer to the southern area of concentration as the northern part of Meso-America.

Meso-America is the region north of Central America in which a process of continuous cultural development has taken place and where there have appeared important urban centers. It is customary to divide this cultural development into three eras: the preclassic (1700-200 B.C.), the classic (200 B.C.-900 A.D.), and the postclassic (A.D. 900 until the landing of the Spanish). Each era is divided into shorter periods.

Since most history and anthropology is documented by men, because men have tended to document that which was outstanding or unusual, because physical evidence about ancient civilizations is limited, and, further, because Spanish *conquistadores* (conquistadors) destroyed much evidence of earlier cultures, it has been somewhat difficult to understand the lives of women in the period before the Aztecs. Likewise, the lives of Mayan women living at the time of the arrival of the Spanish men are also obscured. However, Chicanas have taken strength and motivation in knowing they are descendants of grand civilizations. To understand their strength and motivation, a review of pre-Columbian civilization is warranted. This review reveals the loss of power and stature of women as Spanish colonialism advanced.

Ethnocentrism is a point of view in which people and land are considered "not discovered" until the arrival of the white man. However, significant civilizations did exist in the New World before the arrival of the Spanish-European male. The people in the preclassic period in central Mexico engaged in trade and led a somewhat sedentary life. They had created villages that were probably inhabited seasonally. With the development of a more productive agriculture, the villages became permanent and appeared on the shores of lakes. The people produced ceramics. During this period funerary practices became complex. It is also possible that a process of social differentiation began to develop with the advent of sedentary life. Warriors and priests occupied the upper levels of the social hierarchy. Unfortunately, the material remains that archaeology has to work with offers little information about the social structure of the people. Nevertheless, it can be supposed that blood ties were important and that the concentration of political power in social groups or classes had not yet evolved into that political-social complex we call a state.

In the upper preclassic period the first pyramidal foundations were laid for temples, and hieroglyphic writing, numbers, and the calendar began to be used. These cultural productions undoubtedly reflect the existence of reasonably important cities and of a differentiation between social groups by specialized activities and by political influence. This is probably when the state emerged.

The middle preclassic period is marked by an Olmec influence originating in the Gulf Coast. The figures of this period provide information about physical type, dress, ornaments, cranial deformation, tattooing, hair styles, and body and facial painting. Inhabitants worshipped natural phenomena like rain and sun and fertility. The latter is evident in pregnant female figurines attributed to the Olmec civilization. It is maintained that these were offerings for a good harvest.

Olmecs are documented in the state of Tabasco and the southern portion of the state of Veracruz. Their culture was the earliest of the strongly stratified, or class, societies of Meso-America. (This contention, of course, should be examined to determine if it is the product of cultural biases that look for and find classes and stratification.) Olmec influence was so widespread that it has been considered the "mother culture." Colossal heads, with a high degree of realism, are typical of this culture. Their artistic style produced elongated skulls, resulting from cranial deformation, plus mouths turned down in feline style with the lips curled downward. Olmecs are also credited with having conceptualized the quantity zero.

Olmecs strongly influenced Mayan development. The Mayans maintained a common identity via a common language and some very basic characteristics. They occupied the territory from the Grijalva River in the state of Tabasco in Mexico to the present-day republics of Honduras, El Salvador, Guatemala, and Belize in Central America.

The National Museum of Anthropology in Mexico City (see also Gomez Tagle, Garcia Valdes, and Grobet, *Guide to the Museum*, 1985) contains a Jaina figurine representing a woman with a fine cotton *huipil* (garment), elaborate hairstyle, and facial decoration consisting of scarification on the chin and between the eyebrows. From Yaxchilan, Chiapas, a lintel slab or rock with depictions upon it represents a ruler and woman holding a bundle who are carrying out what has been interpreted as an important transaction. Another lintel, from the late classic period, reveals a ruler of the jaguar linage holding in his hand a scepter. Facing him is a woman, also of high rank, attired in another beautiful *huipil*, offering him the cord for self-sacrifice.

The upper preclassic period reveals more variety in form and decoration. Some places reflect an influence from the northern areas, indicating that people traveled. During this period instruments for construction appear for the first time. Hammers, plumb bobs, chisels, and perforators indicate a high level of technological development.

Speculating what activities women participated in is difficult because of the barriers of contemporary socialization and indoctrination. Thus conceptions, beliefs, and opinions about contemporary gender roles may cloud one's perspective. But a stroll through the National Museum of Anthropology in Mexico City reveals figurines depicting stout, husky people. One small clay figurine of a male holding a ball of dough between his hands is from the middle preclassic period. This probably depicts a propitiatory offering for good crops.

Moving forward in time to the Mexica era, one encounters Xochipilli, the "prince of the flowers." He was the god of song, poetry, theater, love, dance, vegetation, and spring. Sitting on a throne decorated with flowers and butterflies, he wears jade ear plugs, a collar, and sandals of jaguar skin. This figure is very unlike renditions of male figures today. The middle preclassic period reveals the physical characteristics of people at the time as well as their dress, ornaments, and hairstyles. Plaits and locks of hair were common and, it is believed, could have been used either for beautification or to distinguish the user.

A period of great splendor, roughly the seventh century, is the Teotihuacan period. Teotihuacan had approximately 80,000 inhabitants and covered a large area of land. Its planning was outstanding. Streets were laid along the north-south and east-west axes. Houses were built on cement foundations. Scholars maintain that this indicates the existence of a complex social, economic, and governmental system. Adorned tripod bowls with lids are typical vessels. There are many vessels for domestic use: enormous jars for storage, pots for cooking, amphoras with three handles used to carry water, and large braziers for burning incense. There were also large painted buildings with religious motifs. Sculpture incorporated hard and semiprecious stones such as serpentine, alabaster, and quartz. A funerary mask with turquoise, serpentine, and shell incrustation gives no indication of who made it or who wore it (Gomez et al., 1985).

During this late period one also encounters Coyolxauhqui, goddess of the moon, who was sister of Huitzilopochitli, the god of war. Coyolxauhqui is known as "she of the face painted with rattles." This gives rise to her Nahuatl name. Coyolli signifies rattles in Nahuatl, the language of the Mexica, or Aztecs.

The Mexicas founded the city of Tenochtitlan in 1325. By the time the Spaniards arrived two centuries later, the Mexicas controlled a most powerful empire. They were a warlike people who either directly or by commercial means managed to subjugate nations as distant as the Huastecs from the Gulf Coast of Mexico, as well as the Zapotecs and Mixtecs of Oaxaca. The Aztecs collected tribute from the most distant and varied regions. Cocoa beans served as their currency, but most transactions were made in kind. Some of these subjugated people were the first to ally themselves with the Spaniards in order to overthrow the Mexicas.

From this period in Mexican history comes the Sun Stone, or the Aztec calendar, as it is frequently referred to incorrectly. There exists evdence that a female advised the calculation and building of this magnificent instrument. This Sun Stone can also be viewed at the Museum of Anthropology in Mexico City. Not far from the Sun Stone one can see the very large sculpture of Coatlicue, goddess of the earth and of death. She is represented as a decapitated woman from whose neck spring two serpent heads symbolizing streams of blood. She wears a necklace of hands and hearts. Her hands are shown as serpent heads and her feet as eagle claws. Women were represented in Aztec religion as spiritual and mythological figures on earth and in other worlds. The universe was divided into male and female counterparts, and all things were based on male-female elements.

Aztec women played roles in the two important areas of Aztec life: war and religion. They traveled with males in armies into battles. They were cooks and carriers of supplies. Often their ranks were as numerous as those of the armies (Mirande and Enriquez, 1979). Girls received instruction in sewing and embroidery, and they participated in religion. Their studies began very early in life. They were educated in the temples in the rituals of the priesthood and midwifery. They made clothing for the priests and idols, and were taught by elderly priestesses.

Some Chicano studies classes and research concentrate upon Aztec language and culture in Mexico. This area of concentration is included in the pre-Columbian period, which included all New World history until the arrival of Christopher Columbus. The colonial period consists of Spanish settlement through the mid-1800s. It extends geographically beyond Mexico and Guatemala and north into the Southwest of the United States. The third period of study is that of the U.S. war with Mexico. This period encompasses geographically the U.S. Southwest and the Mexican border. It is in this period that Chicano studies tend to deviate from the history in Mexico, Central America, and Latin America to concentrate on the United States.

A fourth period of study is emerging. Concentration on the Americanization of Chicanos and the efforts of activists and resistance spans from 1848 to contemporary times. This period includes the Chicano civil rights movement and the Chicana feminist movement.

INDIAN WOMEN OF THE CONQUEST

When Spaniards came to the New World in the late 1500s, they discovered an advanced civilization. They faced complex and elaborate architecture and an advanced system of medicine and healing. They encountered women and men with dignity and worth, creating art that was incorporated into architecture, and public life. The Spanish men encountered astronomy, elaborate sewage systems, and mass communication among the people they called Indians. They came, bringing with them European motivations and ways of talking, thinking, and behaving.

Often these ways clashed with those of the native people and proved destructive. Sometimes, however, these practices were consistent, providing a basis upon which to build new cultural productions.

From reading most early accounts of the Spanish explorations, one would think it was truly a man's world, that women were incidental, and that at best only one woman, Doña Marina, played a viable part in the ongoing culture of the Indians. Not only is little attention given to the women the *conquistadores* encountered, but little or no mention, except for Queen Isabela, is made of the ones they left behind and the ones who came later—the women of Spain.

Spanish wives, mothers, and daughters remained in Spain to oversee households and plots of land (sometimes large landholdings) and to continue with various forms of business. Some women chose to live together on larger estates. Married women remained in Spain, while their men frequently forgot they were married. Women in Europe might also have conveniently forgotten their Catholic nuptial vows. Because of the nature of the female place in society and the heavy influence of the Catholic faith, this is doubtful, although many jokes remain about chastity belts and the breaking and entering of them.

Instrumental to the arrival of the Spanish men in the Americas was the role of indigenous women. Most closely related to the history and culture of the United States is the encounter of Spanish men with indigenous women in Mexico. These women had lifestyles very unlike the women of Spain. Also, their physical features were different and they were darker in color. Their attire was more casual and colorful, and their lifestyle was defined by other norms and cultural values.

In her early monograph Flor Saiz (1973) discusses the importance of language to indigenous women. This study was repeated later by Martha Cotera in the first nationally distributed text about Spanish-speaking women in the United States. Cotera's *Diosa y Hembra* (Cotera, 1976) focused on the life and history of Mexican-American women. It is still a valuable resource on the lives of pre-Columbian women. Saiz and Cotera along with other Chicanas doing research on Aztec society documented that the Aztecs celebrated the approaching birth of a child with poetry. This was integral with complicated healing and spiritual rituals performed with the new mother and the new child. Medical women would pray as they attended the expectant mother, and the mother would speak to the unborn child in Nahuatl, praising it and telling it of her hopes for its future. Herb teas were boiled and drunk. And upon its birth the child would be presented to the gods.

Some of this early Spanish and Indian history has taken on legendary and mythical characterics, but in the form of sophisticated cultural productions. One female figure straddles the historical periods mentioned above. La Malinche, or La Llorona, appears in the writings of the best Mexican and Chicano authors. She appears in plays, in songs, in poetry. She has been seen by adult women and men. She has appeared to children and old people, to highly educated individuals, the superstitious, the scientific, the religious, and the sacrilegious.

This woman endures the transition into high-tech society. She is the first female to appear in Mexican-American oral tradition as well as in written Chicana scholarship. Her appearance in high-tech society was first reported to me by Martha Cotera. It appears that in the early 1980s Austin, Texas, teenagers would engage in long telephone conversations with their friends. Loud crying and scary noises would interrupt their conversations and parents would tell the teens to hang up the telephone or La Llorona would get them. When my scholarly friend shared this news with me, I became aware that La Llorona is the oldest living female influence in the Americas. She has endured in the Meso-American, pre-Columbian, and colonial periods to contemporary highly technological society. Nowhere else has a female had the experience of La Llorona.

Her Indian name was Malintzin, but the Spanish men baptized her Doña Marina. Even though Hernán Cortés, the man she is most frequently associated with, was the first to be called *malinche*, or traitor, she is now referred to as La Malinche: the woman who betrayed Mexico and made possible the Spanish conquest.

La Malinche is frequently described as Cortés's translator and concubine. The word *concubine* implies that Doña Marina participated in Cortés's adventures willingly. This is questionable. It should be noted that she was barely fourteen years old when she came to be in Cortés's company and that she was a gift from the Aztec emperor.

Many stories have circulated about her, and much controversy surrounds her role in the Spanish conquest of the Aztec empire. Her story, its origin, and its messages have great meaning for the Spanish-speaking people of the Southwest, especially the women and children. The tales of La Llorona have taken on legendary and mythical forms, with enduring and frightening symbolism perhaps not yet recognized.

La Llorona has had more than four different names from four different periods. Malinalli, Malina, Malin, Malintzin, and Ixkakuk have appeared as her pre-Columbian names (Figueroa Torres, 1975), while Doña Marina and La Malinche are colonial period names. From the time of the U.S. war with Mexico to this day, she has existed as La Llorona.

The story of La Llorona symbolizes the stories of three peoples: the Indios, the Mexicanos, and the Chicanos. Perhaps there is a fourth, the people of the spiritual world—that inhabited by the spirit of Aztlan—home of the Aztecs and the current home of most Chicanos.

La Llorona's story has existed as a mixture of myth and reality in the hearts of many Mexican-Americans, even those not living in the Southwest. For them the spiritual trek of the Aztecs into the central valley of Mexico to create the last of the great indigenous civilizations of that country has special significance. It is a life-sustaining significance transmitted to the next generation orally, and women are an intricate part of that transmission. In fact, women play a vital role in the maintenance of the story and the spirit of Aztlan. It is women who can change its negative messages to tell a story of intelligence and courage.

By changing the message, women can address the question: Was Doña Marina a heroine or a traitor? Did she betray her people, or did she save many of them? Mexican and Mexican-American feminists both (including men) have come to the defense of La Malinche. Some feel insufficient evidence exists to determine whether or not Doña Marina performed her services to Cortés voluntarily. Instead of making possible the conquest and then termination of the Aztec empire, she may have saved hundreds, even thousands, of Indians otherwise killed in Cortés's quest for power.

For the Chicanas of Aztlan, to be cultural is to be political. War and manmade boundaries have made this a reality. War and struggle have characterized the Chicana and her people. Thus, Aztlan is a cultural and political place in which to live. It has a relationship to history as a physical and psychological space that has been violated. It is an idea and a behavioral way of life that fights against racism, sexism, and classism.

LA LLORONA AS A CULTURAL HEROINE

The most symbolic and significant aspects of Chicano culture are embodied in La Llorona: She is a female figure, a figure symbolizing the people, the dispossession of their homeland, and the reclamation of their land. People who have left their homeland, as did the Aztecs, or who lose control of it, as did the Mexicans, go through an incredible voyage. In surviving to reclaim their homeland, Chicano people appear to have experienced transformation. Those who appreciate stories about such voyages usually think of the survivor as a hero. However, because society does not attribute heroic deeds to women, it rarely conceptualizes the hero as female. In fact, it does the opposite, producing negative images of women. Since heroines are rare in American culture, and Chicanos in that culture have been Europeanized and Americanized, Chicanos have failed to recognize their cultural heroine and have instead been taught to believe the Euro-American conquerors' version of La Llorona. They are blinded to the heroic deeds of Malintzin.

Today La Llorona is a spiritual, mythological figure, and some claim to have actually seen her. In keeping with Indian tradition, many Chicanos believe in the reality of spirits. Even some psychiatrists will admit that if one believes a thing real, it is real, at least to the believer. In construction such a reality, one not only possesses a cognitive notion of its existence, one behaves as if it were real and gives to it material properties. In this way the story of La Llorona mixes history, fantasy, and spirituality and is believed. It establishes the history and the origin of Mexican-Americans.

Contrary to popular stereotype, Chicano culture is not as male dominated as some would like to believe. One should not surmise, however, that it is matriarchal. Research by Lea Ybarra (1977, 1982a, 1982b) and Maxine Baca-Zinn (1975a, 1975b) suggests that perhaps it is more egalitarian than the dominant Anglo culture. However, the more urbanized and Americanized the Chicanos become, the lower the status of their women falls.

Most women who have deviated from prescribed gender roles have discovered that there are no role models or mentors, and the consequences can be devastating. On their voyages their enemy has been the invisible force of sexism. For minority women an additional enemy has been racism. Be they seen or unseen enemies, the controlling forces of oppression are absorbing. Yet, though oppressive, an enemy can stimulate creativity and alternative thinking and learning, for oppressors require unusual responses from the oppressed. For the oppressed this creativity is often based upon the need to survive. This need has guided the Chicana on her voyage, in which she has created some inspiring coping and living mechanisms that will be discussed in later chapters.

THE LEGEND

The indigenous Aztecs came from Aztlan, far to the north of the central valley of Mexico, where the environment created a synthesis of the entire country and where the story of La Llorona begins. Aztlan existed before there were national boundaries. It is included in the vast northern Mexican territory explored and claimed by the Spanish, but it does not begin there. It goes back further in time, perhaps to a time when humans lived in caves, when they relied upon hunting and gathering, when they had domesticated corn, lentils, and millet. This is a timeof Indians, indigenous people, people with origin in the land; a barbaric time, some would say. I would not. Perhaps the origin of the Aztecs is in the Mesa Verde area among the Anassi and the cliff dwellings in the four corners where the state lines of New Mexico, Arizona, Colorado, and Utah meet.

In 1300 B.C. the Anassi mysteriously left this site, virtually to disappear. Some scholars contend that they migrated south along the Rio Grande and settled among other friendly Indians. The most hearty of them adhered to a saga that guided them to continue to wander until they saw the sacred symbol of an eagle perched on a cactus with a serpent in its mouth. Only when they saw the sacred sight would they settle. Then rag-torn and tattered Indians survived to build the last of the grand civilizations of Mexico in the central valley. La Llorona has her origin in the glory and conquest of this empire. But her name then was not La Llorona. Her name was Malintzin. She was basically an intelligent, multilingual person who had learned to speak many languages as a young child. She had traveled throughout the Aztec empire many times, for her father was a representative of the court of Moctezuma and frequently took his wife and child with him on his duties. Some scholars suspect that Malintzin might even have been Moctezuma's niece. When her father died performing court duty, her mother remarried and had another child, a son. Because the firstborn child, regardless of gender, inherited parental wealth, her mother and stepfather decided to trade Malintzin to another tribe. It appears that Malintzin was traded several times and thus learned the cultural ways of other indigenous people.

In the 1500s the Spanish-European emerged on the continent for the purpose of exploration, claiming new land, acquiring silver and gold, and spreading the teachings of Christianity. To achieve this, they first had to conquer the mighty empire. But they could not do it alone. Hernán Cortés led Spanish soldiers and thousands of Indians in the conquest.

Before the Spanish came upon the Aztec empire, the Mayans, in another area of Mexico known as Meso-America, heard a woman weeping. Sometimes she cried out a warning that something terrible was about to emerge emerge upon the land. Heeding her warning, the Mayans are said to have retreated into the forests of Yucatan and thus escaped most of the brutality of the Spanish influence. Moctezuma got word of the premonition. When in 1521 the presence of Cortés's ships was recorded and messages sent to Moctezuma, Moctezuma became gravely concerned. His court debated whether the ships signaled the return of their plumed serpent god Quetzalcoatle or were a presence unknown. As the Spanish emerged on the land, the controversy escalated. The powerful

Cortés was light skinned, as was the god Quetzalcoatle. Some thought Cortés was indeed the returning Quetzalcoatle.

Moctezuma was in a quandary. He did not know what to think. To secure all his options, he sent a peace offering of many precious tapestries, gold and silver jewelry, and other valuable articles. He sent quetzal plumes, the most precious Aztec possession, and he sent Malintzin, who was one of twenty other women.

Cortés did not receive these women in the same spirit in which they were given. Moctezuma sent the twenty as a peace offering to provide communal services for Cortés's men. Cortés, however, as a European with notions of private property, assigned each woman to a specific man under his command. Malintzin was not originally assigned to Cortés. She was delegated to another soldier who later told Cortés she knew several indigenous languages and was learning to speak *castellano*, the form of Spanish spoken by the men who were mostly from Extremadura, in Spain. Cortés, being the sophisticated military man he was, took Malintzin for himself and used her to obtain information about local geography, as well as to find out about the ways of the land and its people.

Cortés had the women baptized and their Indian names changed to Spanish names. Malintzin was baptized Doña Marina. However, in Mexican history she became known as La Malinche, the traitor, although originally Cortés had been called the traitor by the Indians because they never knew whether he would keep his word or not. As history progressed and was documented in the male-dominated tradition, it recorded Doña Marina as the traitor, rationalizing that her services were voluntary and that male charm and intelligence had made it possible for Cortés to conquer Mexico.

LATENT AND MANIFEST MESSAGES

Granted, Malintzin rendered a valuable service, but Cortés also motivated several thousand Indian men, with their various tribal animosities toward the Aztecs, in conquering the mighty empire. With his horses, guns, and armies, Cortés was able to achieve his purpose: the subjugation of the empire. It is speculated that Malintzin was not only a slave but also a woman with nowhere to go. Malintzin might have remained with Cortés, because she had no options, doing what was necessary to stay alive. Like her, many Jewish women in German concentration camps during World War II were trapped, and to stay alive, perhaps, cooperated with the enemy. This lack of options is horrendously demeaning to women, who suffer as a result.

According to Bernal Díaz del Castillo (1963), Malintzin was a gentle, loving spirit. Bernal Díaz del Castillo, a soldier who was actually on the conquest, maintains that Malintzin forgave her mother and stepfather and asked Cortés to be lenient with them. She said to them that God had been very gracious in freeing her from the worship of idols and making her a Christian. She went on to say that this same god had given her a son by her lord and master Hernán Cortés, and that she had a husband, Juan Jaramillo. She would rather serve her husband and Cortés than do anything in the world. Malintzin could have been brainwashed, or the need to survive so great, that she resigned herself to a Christian way of living and believing. She may have wanted to end oppression by giving in to it.

There is a point in the historical account of Malintzin where history leaves us and fantasy emerges. It is reported that Cortés and Malintzin had a child and had to return to Spain. He wanted to take the child with him. This hardly makes sense, for intercourse with Indians was considered sodomy. It may be that baptized Indians were in a different category. Nonetheless, since, according to Díaz, Cortés had a wife in Spain (and he also had a mistress in Cuba to whom he had promised marriage), there is little credibility in this report.

Rather than part from her son, Doña Marina is said to have drowned the boy. To understand why a mother would kill her child, one must question the assumption that all women love their offspring and want them to live at all costs. More germane here is the Indian contention that humans have spirits and that when humans die, the spirit must also rest. The worst thing that could happen to an Indian was to die away from his or her own land. Given this belief, Malintzin feared that her son would surely die in this far, foreign land. His spirit would thus never rest. Rather than have his spirit cast into eternal damnation, Malintzin committed the ultimate sacrifice and drowned her child, thereby keeping his spirit in his own land and laying it to rest.

One account of Malintzin's end relates that when Malintzin arrived in heaven as the Christian Doña Marina, God would not allow her to enter through the golden gates until she returned with the soul of her child. Malintzin, it is said, had drowned the child in a river. (Southwestern Chicanos contend it was the Rio Grande, but Hernán Cortés and his men never traveled that far north.) The soul is said to have floated away.

Another account tells that when Doña Marina died and went to heaven, God, Jesus, or Saint Peter (who is in this role depends on who is telling the story) would not allow her to enter until she returned with the soul(s) of her drowned child (the bias of the teller affects the tale of La

Llorona). Doña Marina laments that she cannot get into heaven. She wails as she wanders the river, its tributaries, and the ditches, as La Llorona. In a neverending quest, she wails a frightening cry as she painfully searches throughout the Southwest in both physical and mental anguish, attempting to retrieve the soul of her child.

IMPLICATIONS OF THE STORY OF LA LLORONA

La Llorona is savage and cunning. Although she searches for the soul of her child, she will grasp the soul of any person. She is determined to get into heaven and has gone beyond haunting rivers and ditches. She also haunts the forests, graveyards, dumps, cemeteries, railroad yards, and disreputable places.

The story changes from region to region, taking on local characteristics. The number of children La Llorona killed changes. The manner in which they were killed changes. Some say she drowned the youngsters. Others simply say that she killed them. Sometimes La Llorona is an old, ugly woman dressed in heavy black clothing. Sometimes she is a beautiful woman dressed in a flowing, white gown. Some maintain that if one sees her face, she changes into a skeleton, a horse or a goat, or a decrepit old female. She is reported to live in several states, but in each region the color black and old women symbolize the negative. White and young are more palatable. In either guise, La Llorona remains a woman not to be trusted, a woman deviant enough to kill, steal, and try to cheat her way into heaven.

The story has many messages, especially for Chicanas. It speaks to the social implications of motherhood and murder, especially that of children. It also speaks to the implications of premarital sex and community status. La Llorona never married. Her child or children were illegitimate. Some Chicanos of the Southwest believed that the Catholic church views illegitimacy in the same light as murder: as a mortal sin. This view of illegitimacy, currently changing, most severely affects the unmarried mother, who faces social and spiritual consequences such as scandalous talk, scornful treatment, and even ostracism and the penalty of hell upon death. The effects of illegitimacy also stigmatize the child. Until recently, children born out of marriage had no birthrights, and were called bastards and other names.

Many Chicanos do not make the connection between Doña Marina and La Llorona. Those who do, believe that the Christian god was angry at Doña Marina for having engaged in an illicit affair and for having thereby conceived and killed an illegitimate child. Thus she was not let into heaven. Her punishment was eternal damnation. This damnation is relentless, worse than hell, which is a definite place. Some feel she was sent to La Chingada and that she will never retrieve the souls of her dead children. Eternal damnation is actually an Indian concept nonexistent in Catholic Christianity. However, the idea of damnation is also rooted in the idea of sin, a Christian concept. Such a melding of ideas is representative of Chicano, mestizo culture.

A part of the story is missing. In the true form of the abnegating mother, Malintzin gave up her own spirit to eternal unrest rather than allow that of her son's to wander. She serves as the ideal role model of the self-denying female, enduring hardship and unrest. Her image has led to the expectation that women, mothers—in this case, Chicanas—exist to serve, protect, and nourish others. This view, especially, has caused great distress for contemporary women who have absorbed Anglo values of individuality and upward mobility.

AN ALTERNATIVE ANALYSIS

La Llorona deserves a more realistic image than she currently has. The facts require reinterpretation. For example, little attention is given to the fact that Cortés was a willing party with more power and influence than Malintzin. The social message of the story supports a double standard that warns women, not men, against illegitimate childbirth, premarital sex, or sex without marriage. In the narrative Cortés drops out of sight and bears no consequence for any of his deeds. Thus, the story gives strong support and prescription for both genders. It not only prescribes appropriate female behavior and relates the consequences of inappropriate behavior but also grants men certain undebated privileges. There is no sensitivity for behavior dictated by the social circumstances of women living under the pressures of male domination. Male domination is further supported by the oppressing influence of the patriarchal church. Its doctrine evidences extreme social pressure exerted on women to stay well within a defined gender role.

In traditional culture, males have been given certain entitlement because they are born males, and one of these privileges includes not being questioned or confronted by women. Doña Marina tells Cortés she does not want the child to go to Spain. She steps out of her prescribed gender role and is severely punished. It is interesting to note that Cortés does not exert the punishment. A superior being distills the punishment. Thismore firmly plants fear of deviating from the prescribed gender role and fixates La Chicana into that role.

Another idea to be reevaluated is that of homeland. To Chicanos, remaining on or revisiting the homeland is important, whether in life or after death. Note that Malintzin never leaves her homeland: Aztlan, Meso-America, and all of Mexico. She remains if only as a spirit, alive in the world, a legend in Mexico and the United States both. Unlike Malintzin, La Malinche, and Doña Marina, who never visited Aztlan or the Southwest, La Llorona is everywhere they were. In an ironic way the symbolic mother of mestizos, Chicanos, and Mexicanos reclaims the homeland, and this is a heroic, political act.

In the 1960s Chicanos symbolically and in some very real, material ways tried to reclaim Aztlan. Some went as far as arming themselves. There was talk about secession of the Southwest from the United States. Aztlan emerged as the battle cry of the Chicano civil rights movement. The movement, however, was not without its problems, among which were sexism and racism.

THE MESSAGES

Continuing with the legend of La Llorona will lend some insight. Some people say La Llorona will steal any child, kill it, and take its soul in an attempt to fool God and gain entrance to heaven. This version of the story tends to depict La Llorona—and thereby all women—as evil, cruel, cheating, and, in general, immoral and unethical. Men also appear to be dishonest, disloyal, and sexually promiscuous; but implied in how the story is told is that all is the woman's fault. She bears responsibility for the male as well as for herself. The legend presents very negative views concerning both males and females, but it uses a woman in particular to scare children. On the positive side, it does keep youth away from cemeteries, dangerous rivers, and irrigation ditches where they might drown. It gets them home before dark and keeps their telephone use manageable.

La Llorona can serve as a symbol of dignity, value, and worth. She is strong, human, and loving. She loves pragmatically when she will not allow Cortés to take their child to Spain. She knew the Spaniards were different from the Indians; Spain would be a strange place, and her son would surely die on the long voyage or in that strange and different land. Malintzin knew that if her son died away from his own land, his spirit would never rest. She killed her child to save his spirit from an indigenously prescribed eternal damnation, one she endured at the Catholic hand of the Spanish men who believed she murdered her son, a most atrocious crime for a woman.

In keeping with the idea that the Chicana's life has been shaped by the war and violence of men, one has to note that Chicanas are descendants of the conqueror as well as of the conquered. They remain conquered in their homeland, and their status, power, and prestige have changed as the politics of men have changed at the national and international level. It is important to note that they have been symbolically vindicated by the spirit of the Indian woman who was forced to interrelate with the conqueror. A strategy for decolonization is to allow women to share the leadership and to learn and teach the coping mechanisms that Chicanas have developed to deal with centuries of oppression.

Unlike the stereotypical woman who symbolizes fertility, nurturing, peace, and the triumph of Christianity, La Llorona emerges scorned, castigated, and apparently unsuccessful in her search. Firmly believing in the cultural myth and accepting the negative image La Llorona projects thus, Chicanos have not changed this attitude. Thus, the story does not change. It is expected that when the circumstances of women change, the story will change and so will the negative attitude. La Llorona reclaims Aztlan but also keeps alive the spirit of eternal struggle among the last Aztecs until history is set right. The Chicana movement has striven to overcome such conditions, but it has also striven to sustain the wonderful elements of rich Chicano culture. The problem, however, has been a cultural attitude consistent with female oppression. It is suggested that if Chicanas want to change the image of women, one place to begin is by changing the story of La Llorona.

The conquest of Mexico by Spanish males significantly changed the lives of Indian women. It also introduced Spanish women to the New World and developed unique ways of living. Indian women once reigned as goddesses. After the conquest, however, they wore the facial brands of slavery and were subjected to the imposition of a single, male, Christian god. Spanish women, on the other hand, had already been indoctrinated into white, male-oriented Christianity by the time they arrived.

REFERENCES

Baca-Zinn, Maxine. 1975a. "Political Familism: Toward Sex Role Equality in Chicano Families." *Aztlan: Chicano Journal of the Social Sciences and the Arts* 6 (Spring): 13-26.

_____. 1975b. "Chicanas: Power and Control in the Domestic Sphere." *De Colores*, Vol. 1, No. 3: 19-31.

Cotera, Martha. 1976. *Diosa y Hembra*. Austin: Information Systems Development.

Díaz del Castillo, Bernal. 1963. *The Conquest of New Spain*. Trans. J. M. Cohen. New York: Penguin Books. 85-87.

Figueroa Torres, J. Jesús. 1975. *Doña Marina: Una India Ejemplar*. Ed. B. Costa-Amic. Mexico, D.F.: B. Costa-Amic.

Gomez Tagle, Silvia, Adrian Garcia Valdes, and Lourdes Grobet. 1985. *National Museum of Anthropology: Mexico*. Trans. Joan Ingram-Eiser. Mexico, D.F.: Distribución Cultural Especializada. 27-39.

Mirande, Alfredo, and Evangelina Enriquez. 1979. *La Chicana: The Mexican-American Woman*. Chicago: University of Chicago Press. 17.

Saiz, Flor. 1973. *La Chicana*. Denver: La Chicana Publications.

Ybarra, Leonarda. 1977. "Conjugal Role Relationships in the Chicano Family." Ph.D. dissertation, University of California, Berkeley.

______. 1982a. "When Wives Work: The Impact on the Chicano Family." *Journal of Marriage and the Family* 44 (February): 169-78.

______. 1982b. "Marital Decision-Making and the Role of Machismo in the Chicano Family." *De Colores*, Vol. 6, Nos. 1 & 2: 32-47.

Chapter 3

Colonial Women, Women of the Mexican-American War, and Women of the Mexican Revolution

Much of male history revolves around war and violent encounters. Men have made war: women have endured it—then they have nurtured survival and social reconstruction after the trauma. Chicanos have documented their history much the same as Anglo men, who write about outstanding accomplishments of men and the violence they claim built this country. As products of educational institutions that conceptualize and teach history using male-dominated models of superiority, Chicano men have glorified Spanish male accomplishments, conveniently overlooking or minimizing the indigenous experience, and totally neglecting the contributions of women. Chicano history thus makes little mention of the biological and cultural contributions Indian women made to the physical birth of the mestizo race, to which the Chicano belongs, but recognizes the political birth of the Mexican-American.

This political birth of Chicanos, their incorporation into the United States, is generally recognized as a result of the U.S. war with Mexico and the agreement of the Treaty of Guadalupe Hidalgo of February 2, 1848 (Acuna, 1981). Here begins the period of Chicano Americanization. The Treaty of Guadalupe Hidalgo has been the subject of much controversial discussion and certainly deserves attention in the study of Chicanas. Primarily it made Mexican citizens U.S. citizens. (Incidentally, Indians did not become citizens of the United States until the early 1900s.) It also outlined the rights and privileges of former Mexican citizens without attention to gender. In addition, much of the treaty addressed the rights and privileges of Mexicans under Mexican rule. In short, the treaty set down the rules that governed the political life—and by extension the social institutions, of which women were a part—of the Chicano population.

Extending the contention that men make war (and treaties) and women endure it (and them), this chapter first examines the period prior to the U.S. conquest of Mexico, commonly called the colonial period, and then looks at the impact of the U.S. war with Mexico. It considers the position of women in these successive stages of Chicano history, from colonial times, through the war, to Mexico's revolutionary period.

WOMEN OF THE COLONIAL PERIOD

Often periods of historical significance to males are not significant in the same way to women. Mexico following the Spanish (male) conquest was a colonial state. Three hundred years of European colonialism in Mexico demanded both male and female Indian labor. Women worked in the mines. They also provided domestic and sexual services. The tallow for candles used in the rich ore and mineral mines exploited by the Span-ish was the product of their hands. They worked in the silk industry, harvesting silk worms taped beneath their breasts. They toiled in the sugar mills, chocolate mills, and wineries. They were bakers and held many other essential positions in the economy of the time. They were also a source of companionship to men. And for a short time several upper-class Indian women were aligned with Spanish men, at the order of Indian men, in order to keep their households powerful.

Most Indians suffered cultural destruction. Yet some of their beliefs and traditions were integrated into Spanish culture. Gods and goddesses of the earth, the underworld, and the heavens were replaced with concepts symbolized by Jesus and Mary or the devil; indigenous holidays were observed using Christian deities. By 1572 the Catholic friars are reported to have baptized, confirmed, and married most, if not all, of Mexico.

Cotera (1976) notes that after the conquest, thousands of women had their faces deformed. Branding was customary in order to traffic women through the slave market. Married and single women were taken at will. While there were no Spanish women, Indian women still held power as women, for they were a scarce resource. However, as the Spanish women arrived in the mid-1500s, they came to hold the most valued position. Next in status came the criollas–Spanish women born in the New World–and then the mestizas, or women of mixed Indian and Spanish blood. The Indian woman came to hold the lowest social position.

The colonial period in Mexico and in what is now the U.S. southwest was not conducive to the development of increased status for Spanish women. Its forces were employed to maintain women's submissive roles as daughters and wives. In fact, there were few other roles for women. Cotera notes, however, that for a few women it was possible to leave home to direct a school, care for the ill and assist in homes for the destitute, or enter convents. Neither was the colonial period conducive to the well-being of Indians. Much conflict in the United States led to internal quarreling and the enslavement of rivals. However, in 1680 the New Mexico Indians revolted against the Spanish, their politics, and their religion. As a result, the Spanish had to flee to a place near El Paso.

COLONIAL ROLE MODELS

One of the greatest literary figures of the world, Sor Juana Inés de la Cruz, known as "the tenth muse," entered a convent. Sor Juana Inés de la Cruz was the first woman in the Americas to openly question male domination, especially in the Catholic church, which had been a major instrument of colonization and Spanish rule.

There is some disagreement about de la Cruz. Some say she was born a *criolla*, others maintain she was an *española*. Some contend she was born in 1648 (Cotera, 1976). Others say in 1651 (Mirande and Enriquez, 1979). It is known that she continued to produce into the 1690s. She was placed in school at the age of three. De la Cruz advanced far beyond the expectations of a cloistered nun, for by the age of eight she was writing plays and poetry.

From her physically comfortable but socially conflicted life we learn that women were not allowed advanced study. However, her mother cut de la Cruz's hair and allowed her to dress in boy's clothing so that she could continue her studies. De la Cruz incorporated into her writings various areas of social and theological knowledge and physical science. She symbolizes to Chicanas and the world a highly sophisticated, intellectual feminist. Among her writings are *Las Redondillas*, a collection of poems with a specific line scan dealing with male-female issues, and *Contra las Injusticias de Hombre al Hablar de la Mujer* (Against the Injustices of Men's Attitudes in Talking about Women).

COLONIAL WOMEN OF THE NEW WORLD

But the conquest brought other powerful women as role models. One was the image of the Virgin Mary, La Virgen de Guadelupe, the Catholic patron saint of Mexico. Statues and pictures of the mother of Jesus Christ traveled to the New World with the Spanish. In her name, Spanish males destroyed the beautiful native temples to spirits and gods. They looted the remains and constructed in their place colonial churches to the holy mother. In "civilizing" and Christianizing the Indians, the Spanish conquerors emphasized the immaculate conception and the Virgin Mary, after whom women should pattern their lives. The image of the Virgin Mary was touted as proof that the one Christian god was stronger than the many indigenous gods. Sometimes the Indians believed the Spaniards but often they sought only to appease them. When native female deities were consistent with what the Spaniards wanted the Indians to believe, there resulted a cultural blending from which emerged a brown-skinned, Indian-looking Virgin: La Virgen de Guadalupe.

Even though the new Virgin provided much of the basis upon which the Spanish conquerors were able to Christianize and maintain colonization, the power of the church remained concentrated in the hands of men. Therefore sexism was not an issue when Mexico later sought to liberate itself from Spain and, much later, from France.

Among those women of the colonial period worthy of mention are social activists Sor Felipe de Jesús, Sor Antonio Perez de los Santos, Sor Rosa, Sor Antonio de la Santísima Trinidad, and Rosa de Loreto—all Indian women who attended the Convento de Corpus Christi. Also included should be Gertrudis Bocanegra, who organized an effort advocating the education of Indians. She faced a government that saw her actions as unfeminine and threatening. For if Indians learned to read and write, they might revolt.

At the time of Bocanegra, some Indian women were allowed to remain with their families under Spanish rule. These families were to provide administrative structures for their new masters. The devaluation of the Indian female's status continued until the 1700s, by which time the mighty Cacique (Indian rulers) lines were weakened. Women came to serve menial roles as artisans, storekeepers, and farmers. With the construction of convents to house Indian women apart from españolas the Indian woman's role grew even weaker.

Bocanegra was also active in the year of "El Grito de Delores," the cry for Mexican independence in 1810. She organized small underground armies of women, who smuggled supplies into the battlefield. Taken prisoner, she was questioned and tortured. On October 17, 1817, she was executed for not cooperating with supporters of the status quo. Like those of many other women, her activities and contributions went unrecognized for nearly 120 years.

Other women involved in the early Mexican revolutions include Josefa Ortiz de Dominquez, a nineteen-year-old woman known as La Corregidora. During this period women like her performed heroic deeds, and they were not exempt from prison and execution. Other women of interest are Leona Vicario, Juana Beben Gutierrez de Mendoza, Señora Flores de Andrada, Delores Jiménez y Muro, and Guadalupe Rojo de Alvarado. These women were instrumental in establishing revolutionary magazines and newspapers, forming feminist organizations, and fighting in the battlefields. Martha Cotera's *Diosa y Hembra* (1976) and Alfredo Mirande and Evangelina Enriques's *La Chicana* (1979) provide details for the interested reader.

SPANISH COLONIAL WOMEN IN THE UNITED STATES

Some scholars would like to believe that Chicana history is consistent with the female role in family formation. This is not always true. A review of some feminist scholarship gives us insight into community life and business affairs of Spanish colonial women in what now is the United States.

When the conquistadors came, primarily from the area of Spain known as Estremadura (Pizarro was from Trujillo, and Cortés from near Trujillo), they came without women. They found indigenous social structures similar to those encountered earlier in Mexico, but on a different scale. Western communities were subdivided into matrilineages and grouped into clans; and women had important functions at home, on the land, and in the care of ceremonial articles (Swadesh, 1974). Until the U.S. war with Mexico, Spanish women were relatively free on the frontier.

What was happening to women in Spain during this time? Spanish women with families were not to come to the New World until Queen Isabela (La Católica) intervened. She set forth a number of decrees (1536-1751) guiding the moral behavior of Spanish men in the New World. Among the decrees was one stating that men without families, unless they were priests, were not allowed to venture to New Spain (Cotera, 1976). This came as a reaction to the reports of atrocities committed against the native populations, especially against Indian women. Seriously concerned, the queen decreed that only priests and men with families be allowed to go to the hemisphere as her way of addressing the problem.

Spaniards were in the area now known as the United States as early as 1528. The first recorded expedition was Cabeza de Vaca's shipwreck near Galveston, Texas. By 1539 the Spaniards had explored as far north as central New Mexico. Fray Marcos and the black Arab Estevan journeyed through Sonora into Arizona and onto the Zuni villages. In 1540 Francisco Vásquez de Coronado organized his expedition and went into what is now the United States. Rodríguez Cabrillo explored the San Diego bay in 1542. In 1769 Fray Junipero Serra settled San Diego. History has not taught us, however, that the first European women came to the Southwest with the Spanish expeditions. But they did travel with Spaniards and their Indian and mestizo comrades. One woman, on Juan Bautista de Anza's expedition, gave birth to a child on the way to California in 1575 (Cotera, 1976).

It is known that women suffered the long journeys of the conquistadors. In May 1598 Juan de Onate, the husband of the granddaughter of Cortés and great-granddaughter of Moctezuma (Mirande and Enriquez, 1979), guided 210 people from Zacatecas to San Juan de Los Caballeros, near Santa Fe, New Mexico. The troop included men, women, children, servants, and household goods. Only 40 of the original 210 stayed in New Mexico. From 1603 to 1680 small groups of soldiers with and without families joined the original settlers.

Most scholars drop the Indian story here and proceed with the European or Anglo settlement story, but it is important to recognize that the Indian women taught the priests many things about living and planting on the land. How much Indian women taught the Spanish women in whose homes they worked is unknown, but one may suppose their contribution was significant. Indian women taught Spanish women, for example, how to produce finishes on the adobe walls of houses with their bare hands.

Culturally and genetically there was much exchange. The early period witnessed much intermarriage. Some of this came from slave trafficking. Although slavery was outlawed in Spain, it continued to be practiced by the Spanish in the Americas until 1821. So much was the mixing that early Chicano scholar Carey McWilliams (1968) thought the Indian population should be regarded as part of the Chicano population. The populations shared racial background, language, some childbearing and social relationships, and often the Catholic religion.

Spanish activity between 1528 and 1608 produced missions, *presidios* (military compounds), and civilian colonies. The Spanish incorporated some Indian customs and introduced various fruits, animals, architecture, irrigation systems, laws, ranching, and cowboy traditions. Women adopted Indian ways or developed different cleaning and cooking techniques, food storage and preservation procedures, and healing and spiritual approaches. Many of these practices remain alive today throughout the Southwest.

As mentioned, women experienced higher status and relative freedom on the frontier. This was primarily a response to severe conditions; but Frances Leon Swadesh (1974) feels it may also have been a result of early intermarriage between some of the most prominent settlers and the Pueblo Indian women, who had more freedom than their Spanish sisters. Unsupervised women and girls infrequently herded livestock in distant pastures, but they routinely cared for animals grazing in *dehasas* (community-irrigated pastures). Men, however, also worked without women. They were known to do their own cooking in sheep camps and on long buffalo hunts and trading journeys. While their men were gone, women and children frequently ran the farms and ranches.

Mestizo and Indian women took part in butchering and skinning animals, planting crops, irrigating fields, and harvesting. Some elderly and wealthy women were specialists in crafts, herbal medicine, and midwifery. They practiced the healing arts as *curanderas* (healers), *medicas* (doctors), *sobadoras* (masseuses), and *herbalistas* (herbalists). Many a rancher and farmer rode miles and miles to bring the medicine woman with her healing specialty to his family's service. Rooted in ancient indigenous culture, the traditional role of the medicine woman is mixed with Spanish Catholicism and today has taken many women beyond their usual homemaker's role.

Not all frontier women lived on ranches and farms, of course. Some lived or went to work in nearby towns. They worked in hotels as maids; they also worked in laundries and restaurants. A few even engaged in prostitution. Many contemporary Chicanas are descendants of these women and have well-established roots in large cities like Los Angeles, San Antonio, and Denver.

WOMEN DURING THE MEXICAN-AMERICAN WAR

Mexico's independence from Spain (1810-1829), and later from France, plus its subsequent struggle to stay free, weakened its hold over its northernmost territory. Many Mexicans in Texas, New Mexico, and California lost their lives in the struggle to remain a part of the Mexican union. One by one the states fell to the Anglo-Americans and their Mexican collaborators. By February 2, 1848, the Treaty of Guadalupe Hidalgo was agreed upon. One-half of the total Mexican territory was ceded to the United States. This included the states of Texas, New Mexico, California, Arizona, parts of Colorado, and Nevada. In addition, the United States acquired a population of approximately 80,000 people. (Some have estimated the number to have been as high as 350,000.) The territory also included roughly 300,000 Indians. The Indians kept Anglos from effectively colonizing the territory for another forty years.

Common before the war, arranged intermarriage was a way in which Anglo men could obtain Mexican land by becoming Mexican citizens. After the war the practice was necessary in order to allow rich Mexicans to maintain their landholdings.

Anglo colonization posed hardships for many of the former Mexicanas. Cotera (1976) draws attention to Doña Patricia de Leon (1795-1849), one of the founders of Victoria, Texas, who amassed a great fortune. Her story, in part, is the story of many upper-class Mexican families who cooperated with the Anglos. Doña Patricia and her husband established good relations with the president of Mexico, securing a large land grant. They developed the land, using the inheritance brought into the relationships by Doña Patricia. The family collaborated with the Anglo forces, but in the end they were not trusted by the Mexicans and were rejected by the Anglos. They were forced to flee to Louisiana, where for some time they lived in poverty. Doña Patricia returned to Mexico and then returned to Victoria, Texas.

The war had been a bitter conflict, characterized by racism and hatred on both sides. In the end, former Mexicans became subjected to an American way of life that was foreign and oppressive. The study of this period is the study of struggle and conflict. But the war did not create the conflict; it existed prior to the war, and it was rooted in the sexism and racism accompanying the development of the United States.

The U.S. sexist and racist expansionist mentality manifested itself in reactions to the conditions set by the Mexican government to allow Americans to live in northern Mexico. Mexico agreed to the arrangement because few of its people lived in the north. But Americans failed to comply with the conditions and plotted war against Mexico. Part of the plot was to annex Mexico's northern territory and expand the capitalist economy (Acuna, 1981). As time passed, conflicts over the Mexican set of conditions continued. The conflicts became physically and verbally violent until finally war was declared.

Life for new U.S. citizens was well defined in the Treaty of Guadalupe Hidalgo. After the war, there evolved a dual economy with a dual wage system (Barrera, 1979; Blea, 1988). Chicanos were excluded from education, or their education was inferior. Political participation was impossible, and they lost the land (the basis of their wealth). Chicanos suffered religious discrimination, shootings, hangings, and general violence. Many women were raped and otherwise violated. Many believe that the Chicano did not resist. Women, men, and children resisted the hated and feared Texas Rangers. Many of them suffered from the social bandit syndrome (Acuña, 1981; Blea, 1988; Mirande, 1985). Anglos made those that resisted appear as bandits and persons to be ashamed of. Examples of this are Las Corras Blancas in New Mexico, the Espinoza Brothers in Colorado, Joaquin Murietta in California, and Juan Cortina and Gregorio Cortez in Texas. Because men tended to document this history, and because they chose to depict the experiences of men, those of women are at best blurred. Nevertheless, "to the victor go the spoils," and women have always been perceived and treated as part of the winnings in a conquest. This topic is discussed further in Chapter 4.

Americans were so repressive to the new Americans that not until the Chicano movement of the 1960s were Chicanos able to present their side of the story to the American public. Richard Griswold Del Castillo (Garcia *et al.*, 1988) has provided a historical overview of how different Chicano groups have interpreted and used the Treaty of Guadalupe Hidalgo to develop rationales and plans of political action. The Treaty of Guadalupe Hidalgo has also given direction to the lives of women.

WOMEN OF THE MEXICAN REVOLUTION

While Chicanos were being introduced to U.S. citizenship, Mexico continued to develop. As it developed, it continued to affect the lives of its former citizens. Many of the new U.S. citizens still had family and businesses in Mexico. Thus U.S. border populations were greatly affected by the Mexican Revolution and the period of reconstructing the country between 1910 and 1940 (Soto, 1990).

For over twenty years women of the Mexican Revolution have served as role models for Chicanas. Mexican women, referred to as Las Adelitas, traveled with the soldiers in an attempt to win back the land for the peasants. Many of them carried guns and fought in the battlefields. Some rose to high military rank. Most of the women of the revolution, however, cared for family, friends, and neighbors displaced from their homes. They cooked and tended the ill and the wounded. In their daily activities they suffered the hardships of war, but they succeeded in keeping alive many of those involved.

During the revolution it was not uncommon for the women who traveled with the military to collect the corn that fell from the feed sacks of horses in order to make tortillas. It was also not uncommon for them to use for medicine what scarce food sources they had. Many of them gave birth, rested an hour or two, and then, with their babies in their arms, caught up with the forces that had moved forward. Many of those women were assisted by other women familiar with the healing traditions inherited from their Spanish-European and native Indian ancestors. Fifty years later Las Adelitas and the spirit of revolution motivated Chicanos and Chicanas to address conditions of conquest in the Chicano movement of the 1960s.

On a trip to Mexico City in 1985, I had a chance to meet with some of Mexico's leading female and male feminists. They felt that U.S. women should not place such a high value on La Adelita or the *soldadera* (woman soldier) as role models. They maintained that most of these women were camp followers reacting to the male military decisions. They suggested that U.S. women place more value on the life of Sor Juana Inés de la Cruz, the feminist nun who seriously questioned the leadership of men and their violence toward women. Perhaps the Mexican feminists are correct, but there are many approaches to liberation from oppression, and women should be free to choose their own role models for whatever reasons. Chicanas have adopted women of the Mexican Revolution, as well as Sor Juana Inés de la Cruz, as role models. They see their battle for liberation as practical and academic.

REFERENCES

Acuna, Rodolf. 1981. *Occupied America: A History of Chicanos*. 2nd ed. New York: Harper and Row.

Barrera, Mario. 1979. *Race and Class in the Southwest: A Theory of Racial Inequalities*. South Bend, Ind. : University of Notre Dame Press.

Blea, Irene. 1988. *Toward a Chicano Social Science*. New York: Praeger. 102.

Cotera, Martha. 1976. *Diosa y Hembra*. Austin: Information Systems Development. 24-29.

Griswold del Castillo, Richard. 1988. "The Chicano Movement and the Treaty of Guadalupe Hidalgo." In Juan R. Garcia, Julia Curry Rodriguez, and Clara Lomas, eds., *Times of Challenge: Chicanos and Chicanas in American Society*. Houston: University of Houston Press, Mexican-American Studies Program, Monograph Series No. 6. 32-38.

McWilliams, Carey. 1968. *North of Mexico: The Spanish Speaking People of the United States*. New York: Greenwood Press. 67, 80.

Mirande, Alfredo. 1985. *The Chicano Experience: An Alternative Perspective.* Notre Dame: University of Notre Dame Press.

______. 1987. *Gringo Justice.* South Bend, Ind.: University of Notre Dame Press. 9.

Mirande, Alfredo, and Evangelina Enriquez. 1979. *La Chicana.* Chicago: University of Chicago Press. 46-52.

Soto, Shirlene. 1990. *Emergence of the Modern Mexican Woman: Her Participation in Revolution and Struggle for Equality 1910-1940.* Denver: Arden Press. 31-138.

Swadesh, Frances Leon. 1974. *Los Primeros Pobladores.* South Bend, Ind.: University of Notre Dame Press. 9.

Chapter 4

Americanization: Loss of Female Power and Prestige

This chapter explores how the social and political policies during the period of U.S. Americanization after the war with Mexico disempowered La Chicana and caused her to become alienated from her Indian heritage. The disempowerment and alienation are traced in legal proceedings and through the internalization of racist social practices. This chapter incorporates how Chicano and Chicana stereotypes emerged and today are manifested in sexist and racist jokes based upon distorted folklore, traditional customs, and cultural values.

AMERICANIZATION AFTER THE WAR

Very little is written about how Chicanas endured the years of Americanization. A review of this period reveals that women suffered the atrocities of the conquest and the internal colonialism established after the war. Many women were raped. Many also lost land and resources, which cumulated in a severe decrease in quality of life.

The male-dominated Catholic church, built upon the mission system, cooperated with the new government in Americanizing and thereby destroying any nationalist or cultural foundation that existed. Many new Euro-American churches were built during this time. Acuna contends that these new houses of worship provided sanctuary for the racism that coincided with the arrival of thousands of North Americans to California. The church replaced its leading officials with non-Mexican officials. Stricter tithes and an increase in the number of parochial schools resulted, and priests were encouraged to discourage Mexican-American parishioners against rebellion.

After the U.S. war with Mexico, Spanish-speaking people encountered a new economy, one requiring capital. To earn money, men laid track as the railroad expanded. Women witnessed the hard labor and suffering of their men, and nursed them to health after various industrial accidents. They themselves went to work in the many factories built. Both women and men were hanged. Agriculture grew to be big business, and women and children worked long hours in the sun of many fields, as well as in the laundries and white-owned kitchens. Education and the public schools were booming; they were the primary force behind teaching young Chicanas how to be good Americans.

In these schools young women learned how to be neat and ladylike, the American way. They were taught to speak, read, and write English only. They learned to make and wear American clothing, eat American foods, salute the flag, and celebrate the Fourth of July. Some Mexican-American women grew up to be teachers, American teachers. They became instruments of cultural and national oppression without knowing it. They did so in the name of education and helping the Mexican-American citizen acquire a better way of life. The sociocultural forces behind this Americanization effort were so intense and so successful that to question the premise, even today, is to be un-American.

One can be sure something serious is happening when it is manifested in linguistic expression. Racial stereotypes and sexist slurs were common at this time. Women's names were changed: Margarita was now Margaret, Maggie, or Marge. Beatriz was now spelled Beatrice and pronounced differently. Names like Encarnación (incarnation) ceased to be used. Mexican-American women were made to feel so ashamed of their Mexican names that they themselves changed their names. When they had children, many parents gave their offspring Anglo names or Anglicized Mexican names. Dorotea became Dorothy. Elena became Helen, and María became Marie. It was not until the 1960s and the Chicano civil rights movement that these trends began to turn around.

During the Americanization phase, Mexican-American women lived two lives: They were Americans in school and other public places and Mexicanas in their homes and Chicano communities. They had public lives, as well as private lives in the barrios that had sprung up around manufacturing enterprises. Many Chicanas grew up in company towns (Blea, 1990). For many, to grow up during the period of Americanization was to engage in a struggle between what was taught at home and what what was taught in school, for their mothers were of a different generation, a different country, a different historical period.

By the end of the nineteenth century, other ethnic groups shared in the Americanization experience. Northern and southern Europeans were immigrating to the United States. They, like Mexicans, were a cheap source of labor and so were often used against Mexicans to fragment strikes and boycotts against the relentless capitalists.

CHICANAS AS HEALERS

In public and in private Chicanas worked through and endured the transition period. At home they had the most power in the form of childrearing, food preparation and nutrition, spiritual guidance, and cultural information. They adjusted to having men away for many hours but returning dead tired at night. In New Mexico and other places they tended to what was left of the land and their homes on little or no money while the men traveled to places like Wyoming to shear sheep or harvest produce. One area of strength was the practice of holistic medicine in their homes.

Cotera highlights the Americanization period's social climate and the reaction to Mexican-American women in the writings of Susan Magoffin, one of the few Anglo women to come into the Texas-New Mexico area with the Anglo conquerors. She was totally disgusted when she viewed Mexican-American women dancing and smoking unashamedly. Anglo women were not allowed to do this.

Cotera notes another woman of particular interest, the notorious La Tules. Her real name was Gertrudis Barcelo, and she was a successful businesswoman much respected by the local people. However, Anglo women were scandalized by her independent ways. For Doña Tules was one of the best Monte dealers in the Taos-Santa Fe region. She also owned and managed the area's largest gambling hall.

A CHANGE IN STATUS

In New Mexico, especially, one gets a strong feeling for the lives of Spanish women living in the region during the colonial period. Angelina F. Veyna's article "Women in Early New Mexico: A Preliminary View" (1986) reveals the notarial document from Santa Fe and from Santa Cruz de la Canadá. Veyna's work was done in the Spanish Archives of New Mexico, housed at the New Mexico State Records Center, and covers a period from 1710 to 1733, over one hundred years before the signing of the Treaty of Guadalupe Hidalgo.

Veyna found that women were involved in official complaints as both complainants and defendants. They were also able to own property as individuals or collectively with their spouses. Their involvement extended to their inclusion in the distribution of tools, criminal proceedings, power of attorney, estate proceedings, family disputes, land litigation, and personal complaints. Marriages appear to be a legal contract, and marital difficulties were frequently a topic of notarial documents. In addition, the subject of personal honor was also frequently a topic to be settled in the courts.

As the period of Americanization progressed, women were less often represented in court records. During the colonial period, however, legal documents had been initiated by women and against women, whereas later during the period women appeared less frequently. One contention is that public life developed as the domain of men.

Yet during the early Americanization period, colonial practices continued. Although they do not appear to be instrumental in the formation of the legal governing or decision-making body, women were allowed to serve as witnesses as early as the second decade of the eighteenth century. Their testimony appears to have been respected as well as that of men. Perhaps the nature and character of colonial men were such that men were more tolerant of female participation. Perhaps women were more assertive. In Veyna's research there is but one complaint about the negative treatment of women in the courts. The lack of complaints may be because women did not dare complain, or perhaps there was less to complain about. The record is not clear, although there is some historical documentation, like Veyna's, to support maintaining that women had more power.

Widows were a strong constituency. Veyna draws on the work of Janie Louise Aragon (1976), who also notes that in 1790 there was a large widow population. Aragon believes that remarriage by widows was rare. When widows did remarry, they often married older men who died and left them widowed once again. Life was difficult on the frontier, as both men and women died at an earlier age. Perhaps Mexican-American women outlived men.

A focus on marriage during the colonial and Americanization periods must note that the social prescription for marriage was well established in the *Entriega de Novios* (Blea, 1988). This secular custom took place during a marriage reception. The bride and groom were presented to the society as a married couple and in front of this society were instructed on how to behave in marriage. The ritual was a musical composition at the time of presentation, a unique practice, that gave highly egalitarian practical and spiritual advice.

Veyna's preliminary look at will and testament documentation of women living in New Mexico from 1744 to 1767, during the mid-eighteenth century, illustrates some of the material possessions of women (1985). Women owned, purchased, and disposed of property. Some owned and disposed of valuable property in the Rio Arriba region. They owned farm and ranch and carpenter tools, houses, stables, fields, and orchards in various locations. They also owned furniture, items such as chests, stools, tables, benches, and chairs. They owned a variety of clothing: mainly skirts, capes, mantillas, handkerchiefs, stockings, slips, and blankets. Clothing was made of silk, cotton, and piquin. Among decorative items were listed ribbon, lace, and fringe. Some of the women owned musical instruments like guitars and violins. Others owned jewelry. One woman owned seven strands of dark pearls. Another owned a coral-and-silver choker, some blue enamel bracelets, and some exquisite pearl earrings. Women also are noted as owning guns and knives, candles, and food.

Such meticulous records are not known of during the Americanization period. However, it is known that women owned, sold, and otherwise controlled land; and, as mentioned, they were instrumental in the transferral of land by way of intermarriage.

Veyna contends that women's wills also provide insight into the Christian pantheon of the time. Among religious articles owned by women were prayer books, crucifixes, pictures of saints (*retablos* and *cuadros)* and statues *(bultos).* Some of the saints included female images: Santa Isabel, Nuestra Señora del Pilar, and Nuestra Señora de los Remedios.

Livestock seems to be distributed evenly between female and male heirs. In disposing of property, even when male consent had to be secured in these transactions, it appears that it was frequently the woman who made the decision of how to dispose of her own property. It was not uncommon, however, to have each spouse in a marriage claim and dispose of his or her own property. This was done to ensure that materials were not bequeathed to inappropriate heirs. None of the documents, notes Veyna, gave the illusion that women hesitated to specify how their goods were to be distributed.

In spite of the fact that most of the population was illiterate, especially the women, some women were at least able to write their names. Veyna refers to them as forming a part of a literate elite, and indeed this group did exist. In Veyna's court records there is no mention of race or caste. This is perhaps because the Spaniards were the majority population and recorded their own history best.

SPANIARDS AND INDIANS IN THE SAME SITUATION

There is, however, insinuation of class differences by the use of the titles *doña* (high-status female) and *don* (high-status male). Of more importance in court records were other statuses such as married, widowed, or orphaned. In genealogical records of marriage, death, baptism, and *diligencias* (nineteenth-century official testimony before final permission to marry), however, nationality is frequently recorded and reference to *indio* frequently appears.

An area lacking in documentation is the interaction of Indian and Hispanic women outside worker-employer relationships. By the end of the Anglo conquest of the Southwest, the Indians of the Southwest had lost much land, and plans were made to relocate them to reservations. They had been subjected to new illnesses and laws, and many had been killed or starved to death. Some groups resisted Anglo intrusion for a long time. Those who resisted were killed or tried in American courts, where they were found guilty of various crimes. With hardly an exception, an Indian could not win in an English-speaking court if the case made it to court.

The Spanish-speaking population was engrossed in Americanization struggles. They were too busy trying to survive to come to the assistance of Indians. Those who recognized that Indians were also experiencing cultural and physical genocide could do little about it. In addition, historical circumstances and racism had taught many Mexican-Americans not to align themselves with Indians.

However, there are many similarities between what happened to Indian women and Mexican women. Both were involuntarily incorporated into the United States. Both had their people killed in the process. Both were subjected to Americanization. Both had their language and religion degraded and suppressed. Both experienced a change in economic and social status when the Anglo came to the Southwest. However, there were some major differences. Young Spanish-speaking women were not taken from their homes and placed in school, as were young Indian women. Nor were the lives of Mexican-American women formally regulated by a specific body of laws.

SOME HUMOR IS VIOLENT

In my four-year experience of collecting jokes, in Chicano studies I have encountered only one Indian joke featuring a female. This chapter proceeds by exploring how racist and sexist Chicana stereotypes manifest themselves in jokes based on the historical experiences, folklore, traditional custom, and the cultural values of the Chicano population. To preserve here the linguistic tradition, I have not altered the language in which the jokes were recorded. The chapter surveys the role of the dominant society and Americanization as the basis for transmitting stereotypes that work to disempower women. This is a serious endeavor, for stereotypes and jokes cause violent harm to women by contributing to low self-esteem when internalized.

In part, the subject of ethnic or sexist jokes has been considered a moral or ethical issue. In this country the freedom of speech is a fundamental right of all citizens, and thus far there has not been legislation to prevent racist or sexist jokes. Since the massive European immigration in the late eighteenth century and the early nineteenth century, ethnic jokes have been popular in spite of their many opponents.

Where does a joke begin? Occasionally jokes emerge within the disadvantaged population itself, but many Chicano jokes are rooted in differential power relations. Over the years the basic structure of the jokes has not changed much: The dominant group feels free to poke fun at the disadvantaged group. Consider the following example of a Chicano joke based upon the fact that Mexican-Americans lost the U.S. war with Mexico. A major battle in that war was the battle at the Alamo, a small mission in San Antonio, Texas:

> Three men were flying in a plane. The plane was bombed and the men had to parachute out. The French man yells, "Viva la France!" The Native American man yells, "Geronimo!" The Mexican yells, "Remember the Alamo!"

The catch to the joke is that Chicanos are confused and have nothing to be proud about. They are ignorant, without fully knowing their own history. Those who have internalized the Americanized version of their history are wrong in thinking they have inherited the U.S. victory. For Anglo-Americans have chosen to depict the Alamo as a battle they won. They did not. They depict the battle's heroes, especially Davey Crockett, as not only victorious but gallantly brave to the very end. In fact, Davey

Crockett was not at all as portrayed, for example, in Walt Disney movies. He was a mercenary soldier, captured, detained, and executed by the Mexicans. But the joke, its support in the media, in folklore, and in biased history books, upholds that Mexicans are weak and unvictorious, without heroes. This view creeps into the social fabric of society and makes it easier for Americans to discriminate against Chicanos.

Chicanos who are socially conscious and know their own history know the truth about the Alamo and choose to interpret the battle another way. They take revenge by acknowledging that, indeed, they do remember the lies and suffering of the Alamo. They are motivated by this joke to set the record straight and obtain social liberation for Anglo oppression.

Another Alamo Joke is linked to aspects of the Chicano family experience and the Mexican-American fascination with automobiles:

How come only 20,000 Mexicans died at the Alamo?
Because they had only three cars.

This next joke relates how very few people will assist Chicanos when they are in need:

What do you call a Chicano hitchhiker?
Stranded.

One stereotype is that Chicanos are violent and illiterate:

Why do Chicanos wear hair nets?
To hide their knives in.

Why did the Mexican take seventeen of his friends to the movies with him?
Because the sign read "Under 18 not admitted."

A joke about Chicano graffiti:

Why is there no Mexican literature?
Because spray paint only went on the market twenty years ago.

There are cross-cultural racist Chicano jokes promoting Anglo superiority by suggesting ethnics are stupid, lazy, and thieving:

What happens when you cross a Chicano and a Polish person?
You get a person who spray paints chain link fences.

What happens when you cross a Chicano with a nigger?
Their children are too lazy to steal.

Some jokes are based on the ill-perceived physical characteristics of the population:

How many Mexicans does it take to grease a car?
One, if you hit him just right.

Most frequently, jokes are made about language and cultural practices:

What is the difference between select and choose?
Select is when you pick something out, and choose are what a low rider wears on his feet.

Why do Mexicans refry beans?
Because they did not do it right the first time.

Why do Mexicans make tamales for Christmas?
So they will have something to unwrap.

What is long, brown, and has a cumulative IQ of 80?
The Cinco de Mayo parade.

A Mexican fireman had twins. What did he name them?
Hose A and Hose B.

Some jokes combine variables with an economic base:

How do you get fifty Mexicans in a Volkswagen?
Throw a welfare check in it.

What do you get when you put two Mexicans in a shoe box?
A pair of loafers.

Women, regardless of race, class, or ethnicity, hold a disadvantaged position in the power relations of society. Sexist jokes exist about them also:

Never marry a woman until you have seen her mother. Seeing her will tell you what your wife will look like in twenty years.

Some jokes and "humorous" stories imply that women enjoy the victimization of the many violent acts committed against them.

There were two Chicana nuns who had to walk through the woods to get to and from town. They made sure to leave early enough so as not to be in the woods in the dark. One day when they were returning home, it began to get dark and one of the nuns thought that it would be better to go the long way around the woods. The other thought it would be quicker to go through the woods. They were going through the woods, when suddenly two men jumped out from behind the trees. Each forcefully took one nun and raped her, one behind a tree and the other behind a bush. One nun said, "Forgive them, father, for they know not what they do." The other said, "Mine does."

Jokes about Chicano men also exist. For example,

What do you call a Mexican with a vasectomy?
A dry Martinez.

Most international jokes collected in Chicano studies put down Mexico. This one is also cross-gender:

Why wasn't Jesus born in Mexico?
Because God could not find three wise men and a virgin.

Most jokes are cruel, but racist and sexist jokes are the most cruel and disgusting to ethnic and minority women:

Before she lost weight, did you know Oprah Winfrey got arrested in the airport?
She got caught with 30 pounds of crack between her legs.

How do you get a Mexican girl pregnant?
Come in her shoes and let the flies do the rest.

What do you call a Mexican prostitute without legs?
Ground meat, or cum suelo.

What do you call a Chicana who had an abortion?
Crime stopper!

Some stereotypes maintain that Chicanas are dirty, passive, and lazy and that men are entitled to be unfaithful:

Why would a man marry a Mexican woman?
So he can leave home without her.

Why do they have banquets after all Mexican weddings?
To keep the flies off the bride.

Many Americans lament that they live in a violent society in a violent world. Most attention to violence has been given to incidents such as muggings, shootings, and murder reported by the media and to violent fictional productions. Children's toys are criticized for blatant and inadvertently violent messages. Sometimes movies depicting gang violence are boycotted or demonstrated against. However, rarely does the discussion revolve around the violent use of the structure and function of language to demean and discredit minorities and women.

Indeed, rarely do discussions on ethics and morals involve the social use of language and the impact of its use upon the quality of life. Instead, many choose to ignore that some people entertain themselves by degrading and demeaning others. They fail to see that discrimination is a process that begins at the cognitive level with thoughts and ideas transmitted first by means of language, then into behavior. To rectify this, there is need of much social support.

Unfortunately, Mexican-American women have lost the kind of social support they had before the Americanization period. As they have become more urbanized, they have absorbed more Anglo values. They have lost contact with Indian women. Some Chicanos are even repulsed by their own people. The kind of social support that existed in the *Entriega de Novios*, for example, does not exist in Anglo culture. There is no doubt that the social worth of Indian and Hispanic women has decreased as Americanization progresses.

REFERENCES

Acuna, Rodolfo. 1981. *Occupied America: A History of Chicanos* (3rd ed.). New York: Harper & Row. 121-26.

Aragon, Janie Louise. 1976. "The People of Santa Fe in the 1790's." *Aztlán: Journal of International Chicano Studies*, Vol. 7, No. 3:391-417.

Blea, Irene. 1988. "La Entriega de Novios: The Cultural Practice of Being Given and Taken in Marriage." Unpublished manuscript, paper presented at Hispanic Cultures of the Americas Conference, Barcelona, Spain.

______. 1990. *Bessemer: A Sociological Perspective of a Chicano Barrio*. New York: AMS Press.

Cotera, Martha. 1976. *Diosa y Hembra*. Austin: Information Systems Development. 59.

Veyna, Angelina F. 1985. "Una Vista al Pasado: La Mujer en Nuevo Mexico 1744-1767." *Trabajos Monográficos: Studies in Chicana/Latina Research*, Vol. 1, No. 1: 28-42.

______. 1986. "Women in Early New Mexico: A Preliminary View." In Theresa Cordova et al., eds., *Chicana Voices: Intersections of Class, Race, and Gender*. Austin: University of Texas Press.

Chapter 5

Contemporary Cultural Roles

This chapter evaluates the contemporary condition of Chicanas. It considers Chicana experience by age and income and is a precursor to the chapter on breaking barriers. It also explores the characteristics of recent social changes and how they affect women's roles. From their everyday experience emerges a value system and way of life specific to Chicanas, a life manifested in music, literature, art, politics, criminal justice, health, and diverse personal lifestyles.

DIVERSITY AMONG CHICANAS

Chicanas are a diverse population. In some parts of the country more than others to be Chicana means to be influenced by Spanish, Indian, and Mexican cultural factors. Some Chicanas trace their origins back hundreds of years to Europe and the Moorish influence in Spain. More recent arrivals are immigrant women from Mexico, Central America, and South America. They are all ages, sizes, body types, ideologies, educational levels, and economic levels, and they bring with them a variety of experiences. Among the several things they all have in common is the Spanish language and their inheritance of the Chicano colonial experience as well as their endurance of its discrimination.

Chicana diversity means there has also been uneven ideological development among U.S. Chicanas. Most fit into one of four categories. The first three groups are categorized by age; the last, by community advocacy. The age categories are (1) older women, (2) middle-aged women, and (3) young women. Nan Elsasser, Kyle MacKenzie, and

Yvonne Tixier y Vigil discuss these groups when introducing women from New Mexico (1980).

The elder generation tends to be over seventy years of age and consists of women with rural backgrounds who grew up relatively isolated from mainstream society. These women have had to endure four wars: World War I, World War II, Korea, and Vietnam. Those in the work of Elsasser and her colleagues grew up when New Mexico was still a territory and not a state. They, like other women today, were responsible for the emotional and physical well-being of their families and had intense relationships with people in their communities. These women grew up in traditional culture at the turn of the century and have experienced hard physical labor. They speak Spanish.

Their childhood playtime was abbreviated. Their highest educational attainment was eighth grade. Their primary activities were housework and farming. However, a few Chicanas in the older-women category attended college and became teachers in small communities. Most not only had little formal schooling but also had little access to medical facilities; yet they frequently were *medicas* (general practitioners), *sobadoras* (chiropractors), *herbalistas* (herbalists), *parteras* (midwives), or *curanderas* (those who heal at the emotional, spiritual, and physical levels). Those who experienced the holistic approach of the *curanderismo* still remember their treatments and have passed on this tradition. Many of these women have had at least twelve children, for birth control information and practices were rare, and have experienced the death of at least two.

Women in the older-women category tended to be Catholic and married young, at about seventeen years of age (Elsasser, MacKenzie, and Tixier y Vigil, 1980). Many grew up knowing they were going to get married. When they married, they assumed their husbands were going to take care of them. Many of these women today are widowed and, without husbands to take care of them, are poor.

A few older-generation women were politically active. Many were Republicans, especially in New Mexico, but they admit to being Republican because their fathers and husbands were. When their husbands were alive, they voted the way their husbands told them to vote.

These women are the grandmothers and great-grandmothers of the current generation. Some now attend senior citizens centers. Several older women still enjoy planting their own gardens, stringing their own chili, and dancing. They prepare a variety of foods. Like other Chicanas they are versatile. They tell *cuentos* (stories) about *brujas* (witches) and La Llorona. They now live in cities (80 percent of the Chicano population is urban).

The second group of contemporary women is more urban. They tended to move to cities from villages and farms after World War II and are the daughters of the women in the first category. They tend to have work experience outside the home. Although they began working in their late teens and early twenties, for the most part they have been homemakers and mothers. Those with work experience outside the home were prompted to examine the nature of their responsibilities in the home and with family and neighbors. Some women in this middle-aged group were motivated toward community involvement by their experience.

The availability of education and the need for it in a highly capitalistic environment created the third group: young women. This group is the first generation to complete high school and attend college. They still regard their families as one of their primary responsibilities, but they balance this with careers and other interests.

The women of group four consist of those who are poor or working class. Some tend to the welfare of the community through activities advocating social change. They combine the need for change for Hispanics and for women in their work and in their lifestyles. They seek to change social institutions through organized activities via electoral and nonelectoral politics, lobbying, striking, picketing, petitioning, marching, and boycotting. Generally, their activities concentrate in the nonelectoral arena. Sometimes highly visible, their actions can also be individual, private, and often quiet. These women negate simplistic attempts to define human history as a time line only of famous Anglo leaders and great Anglo events.

The women in all four categories call themselves Mexicanas, Hispanics, and Chicanas. Whatever they call themselves, their labels each carry a different ideological framework and mode of expression in literature, music, art, and politics. Yet they hold in common their individual contribution to the contemporary Hispanic lifestyle.

SURVIVING THE DECADE

The 1980s was to be the decade of the Hispanic. Perhaps it was. Chicanos were rarely called Chicanos; some even felt it was backward to use the term *Chicano*. *Hispanic* was the "in" term. Richard Lacayo in a *Time* magazine article in 1988 wrote that the country was taking on a Hispanic flavor, felt in what Americans were eating, in art, in the language, in literature, and in music. Lacayo noted that some developments were difficult to pin down and that they were happening, not because of "aesthetic intelligence," but because the creative work produced by

Hispanics is more and more being recognized as American: Hispanic-American. Lacayo's use of the term *Hispanic* was a bit confusing. He used it in a generic sense to include Mexican Americans, Cubans, and Puerto Ricans.

To build his argument, Lacayo cited examples from women's fashions, "the bolero curve of a woman's jacket," the movies, and the *jicama* (a starchy tuber somewhat similar to a potato) in American salads. Lacayo's article raises the question: What is Chicano culture? If it is shared knowledge, does this trend mean that the United States is now ready to learn what Chicanos know?

The July 1988 special issue of *Time* treats Hispanic culture as homogeneous. It is not. It notes the musical creations of the electric Celia Cruz (a black Latina), who for over forty years has been known as "La Reina de la Salsa" (the Queen of the Salsa). No attention is given to Chicana or Mexican American singers. The issue also notes the creative work and attraction of Brenda K. Starr, Sweet Sensation, and the Cover Girls, plus Linda Ronstadt's mainstream success with her recording of the album *Canciones de Mi Padre*. Cultural diversity was certainly not Lacayo's focus.

In the arts Latinas—women—have also been busy writing poetry, short stories, and novels; painting; designing; and making movies. They continue with the old ways, but they adapt and create alternatives. Their view of the world is beginning to be felt, although it is sometimes difficult for the general public to learn what they are doing because their lives do not attract much print or other media attention.

The new Chicanas have been active in other ways. They have not only been homemakers, taking in boarders, and washing and ironing clothing. They have also been employed outside the home in factories, running heavy machinery, at desks, in classrooms, in hospitals, in courtrooms, in their churches, and in large corporations. They carefully balance their productive lives outside and inside their residences, being constantly watchful for sexist and racist discrimination.

Lacayo is correct when he notes that there was not a time without a Mexican movie, a hacienda-style suburb, or a Latin crooner; and he notes that demographics are the main reason for this change. In 1988 he estimated the Hispanic population to be about 19 million, a 30 percent increase since 1980. Today there are well over 20 million Hispanics in the nation. The figures are misleading because of the large immigrant population that cannot afford to be included in any head count. Hispanics now account for roughly 8 percent of the U.S. population. The majority (63 percent) are of Mexican descent. Puerto Ricans (12 percent) and Cubans

(5 percent) are the next largest groups. The remaining Hispanic population comes from Central and South America and the Caribbean. But even these figures are misleading.

Many Latinos are also black. Although black Latinos see themselves as having access to both groups, they can easily lack credibility with both groups as well as with the Anglo community. A *Hispanic Link Weekly Report* (February 20, 1989) estimates that black Latinos range in number from 290,000 (according to U.S. Bureau of the Census statistics in 1980) to as high as one-third of the nation's 20 million Hispanics. Black Latinos are concentrated in New York, California, and Florida but are found in all fifty states and tend to originate in Mexico, in the Caribbean, and along the coast of South America—areas where native Indians, African slaves, and the colonizing Europeans intermixed. Black Latinos predominate in the Dominican Republic and are also concentrated in Panama, Puerto Rico, and Cuba. Whether they are black or Latino is not distinctly defined, and black Latinos often choose their own classification. No matter which group they choose to identify with, they endure discrimination.

Musical artists Mongo Santa María and Cheo Feliciano are black Latina females, as are businesswoman and consultant Miriam Cruz and Antonia Pantoja, two of the founders of ASPIRA (which means to aspire) and other Latino advocacy organizations. Also, WFSB-TV anchorwoman Bertha Coombes and former Commonwealth senator Ruth Fernandez are black Latinas. It has been estimated that by the year 2000 Hispanics will number 30 million. There has been no projection of the number of black Latinos.

Lacayo's *Time* article estimates that one-third of all U.S. Hispanics intermarry with non-Hispanics. Although most Chicanas marry Chicanos, intermarriage has been somewhat common, although not always acceptable. Women contend that most intermarriage takes place between Chicano males and Anglo females. It appears that males have internalized the media message idolizing the "white goddess." White women are held up as the model of beauty; the kind of woman to lust after and sometimes marry. To some men attachment to such a woman signifies upward mobility and masculine worth, and it leaves the Chicana outside, valueless. Some feminists feel intermarriage is harmful to the community, especially when the male marrying out of the culture is someone with a good education and plentiful resources.

When a Chicana marries an Anglo male she accepts patriarchal defined roles for women of color. Emma Perez (1991) contends that in doing this the Chicana accepts her role as a colonized female in a form of false consciousness that has little benefit to her. These roles get played out in sexual politics. By marrying an Anglo, a Chicana believes she has gained power by marrying up in the social ladder of race relations. Perez conceptualizes this as the sexual politics of miscegenation in the twentieth century and extends her argument to state that la Chicana's sons will also have more social power than she does. The daughters of an Anglo male and a Chicana have the father's white name to insulate them from racism, thereby placing them closer to the power of white men.

The impact of the trend of male intermarriage is devastating not only to Chicana psychology but also to community economics. Resources in the form of children, who may contribute to that community, are also lost in Chicano male-Anglo female intermarriage because children tend to identify with the mother's culture. In addition, most men who intermarry tend to move their families out of the barrio.

ARTISTIC INTEGRATION

Robert Hughes, in the same issue of *Time* (1988), notes that in cultural assimilation of Hispanic artistic traditions into the mainstream, mainstream American museums have only just begun to accept many kinds of art, especially Hispanic art, being created in the United States. Even today this recognition is not shared by everyone. Hughes, who does not review a single female artist (1988), feels the situation has improved since 1969, when New York City's Metropolitan Museum of Art presented what some Chicanos felt was a condescending exhibition entitled "Harlem on My Mind." Most of Hughes's attention was also on the East Coast, but his article does report that the museum was confident that spending $5,544,000 on Velásquez's portrait of Juan de Pareja, his Moorish assistant, would improve the self-esteem of the museum's black and Hispanic public. It did not. Most felt this action to evade American Chicano art, to deny its existence. It was felt to be eurocentric, and a token at best.

Needless to mention, Chicana art does not hang in the Metropolitan Museum or in any other major museum. In fact, Chicano art is rarely represented outside the Southwest; however, many Chicana artists do exhibit in small, Chicano nonprofit galleries whose goal is to make Chicano artistic expression available to the public. In addition, several national Chicano art exhibits have traveled around the country. One of them was produced by Maurene Acosta. Although this exhibit was well received, its image was tarnished because it was sponsored in part by the Coors Corporation, which Chicanos had been boycotting for many years. Another, "Thirty Contemporary Painters and Sculptors," was a show of 180 works on view in 1988 and 1989. Curated by two non-Hispanics and reviewed mostly by non-Hispanic reviewers as the most detailed and serious effort ever made to survey the current painting and sculpture of Hispanic Americans, the show was male dominated.

The latter exhibition brings to the surface a discussion of who controls artistic productions when they become marketable. Anglos have, for example, taken over Native American cultural productions, marketed them effectively to other Anglos, and shared little or nothing with the people they thus exploit. Although few Anglo women have excelled in artistic marketing, neither has it been a strong area for Native American women, nor is it expected to be an area of growth for Hispanic women. Hispanic women may produce, as have native women, but Anglos still control the market.

Chicanas struggle to depict their old and new roles at the community level. Some have even received national exposure. Charlotta Espinoza creates in Denver, Colorado. She and others like her incorporate a feminist perspective into their art. In New York City the Museo del Barrio and the Museum of Contemporary Hispanic Art have long worked to support Chicano art, but women have complained about male dominance.

Most Americans hear the words "Hispanic art" and think of Chicano murals on the walls of buildings in east Los Angeles. This Mexican tradition began in the United States in the 1960s as a means of political and social education of the public; its themes generally addressed the oppression of Chicanos. The murals were also decorative. Hughes notes that to assume that Chicanos paint only murals is to assume that women's art follows the form of Judy Chicago's "The Dinner Party" and is the chief work of art produced by American women. The point to be made here is that Chicana art is not like Chicano (male) art and not like Anglo feminist art. It is sometimes a mixture of the two, and it frequently has strong cultural influences.

Hughes notes that the United States has no shortage of first-rate Hispanic artists who work out of deep convictions and connections to their Latino, religious, and ideological heritage. The same is true of Chicanas, though they are mostly circumscribed to Hispanic art shows or into "minority" shows, which ghettoize the artist. An interesting paradox is that a minority artist who "makes it big" is not always thought of as Chicano.

As Hughes notes, American art took a long time to evolve. Much time was spent idealizing European art, perhaps because the United States has always had a cultural inferiority complex about not being European. It has not yet accepted itself for what it is: A nation of diverse cultures, one in which women have participated.

POLITICAL COURTSHIP

Some people do not like Chicano art because it is political. Some of it is indeed political because politics is a serious concern for Chicanas and Chicanos. Only recently have politicians begun to court the Chicano vote, yet the power elite allows Chicanos no control in any area of politics. The increasing number of Latinos has been a source of political support and power to which politicians—Chicano and otherwise—have turned. For them, numbers translate into votes, votes translate into power, and power translates into victory and a better quality of life.

Chicanas have been a viable part of the political, electoral and nonelectoral, struggles. To take part in this endeavor required overcoming the stereotyped idea that women were not political. Chicano males believed women were not competent enough to handle political struggle and thought. Their blinders did not permit them to see that by their side women had survived several wars, rebuilt homes and communities, maintained culture, and organized multipurpose organizations.

So strong was this feeling that 1980 also saw the rise of English-as-the-official-language bills in several states. This was a reaction to the increasing numbers and power of Latinos. It was also an attempt to maintain the status quo of white power. In 1982 the United States also saw new Chicano Democrats in the House of Representatives. In the four-year period between elections, Latino representation in Congress also increased, doubling the number of Hispanic voting members in Congress (Sierra, 1986). At the state and local level the number of Latinos in elective office doubled from 1973 to 1984. Part of the battle was to hold onto the seats gained by Chicanos in state elections in the mid-1970s. Chicanas did not occupy many of these seats.

Christine M. Sierra asserts that greater electoral success at the local levels can be attributed partly to the fact that Chicano political experience generally evolves from the community level. In addition, Chicanos may be more interested in local concerns than national or international issues. The size of a political unit and the percentage of Chicanos in it also explain Chicano electoral success.

Sierra draws on the work of John Garcia (1983) to find that when Chicanos comprise a small percentage of a community (less than 10 percent) or are the majority group within it (65 percent and more), their chances of winning elective office increases. At this point they either represent a nonthreatening token, an acquisition of power, or individual upward mobility. No studies on how Chicanas gain power have been done. Perhaps they gain power by a combination of the above factors and their work in their community.

The 1980s also produced some measurable gains in Chicano politics. There were gains in representation as a result of increasing numbers and pressure-group politics. These efforts sought to ensure Latino interest when reapportionment of state and congressional districts, based on the 1980 U.S. Census, took place. Many of these groups also fought for the extension of the Voting Rights Act in 1982 and against English-as-the-official-language bills in several states.

The underrepresentation of Latinas in elected office is most glaring. Although a few are found in state legislatures, no Latinas sit in Congress. In 1982 California, the largest Latino-populated state in the union, had no Latina state senators or representatives. Although this has changed, by 1985 only 12 percent of all elected positions held by Latinos throughout the country were held by women (Sierra, 1986).

In 1989 former state senator Polly Baca from Colorado, who was the strongest Chicana elected official and who comes from a political family, lost her National Democratic Committee vice-chair position after eight years in office. Two years before that she had given up her post as state senator to run for Congress. She was defeated by an Anglo male. Baca maintains that her opponent outspent her; and, indeed, money is a factor in most elections. However, grassroots organizing has been the most effective Chicano strategy, and Baca was good at that. Perhaps the people of her mixed Anglo-Chicano district were not ready for a Chicana in Congress.

This trend is consistent with the level of political underrepresentation of all women in the United States. Combined class, race (ethnicity), and gender biases inherent in the social and political systems underlie the political underrepresentation of Chicanas. This combination causes Chicanas to face special obstacles in penetrating public spheres of power dominated by Anglo and minority men. Chicanas share with other women male stereotypes, childbearing and -rearing responsibilities, and fewer economic resources.

THE NATURE OF CLASS AND MARRIAGE

There is an income differential among Chicanas. Many poor Chicanas are to be counted among those enduring the feminization of poverty; but there are many working-class, middle-income, and higher-income Chicanas as well. Most are working class, however, and those with higher incomes are married to working husbands. Cultural variables in the selection of marriage partners cut across class and are more consistent across gender, even though there is a woman's culture.

Throughout the Southwest the poor and the working class tend to live in overcrowded, deteriorating homes and apartments and varyingly suffer from the physical exhaustion of overwork and undernourishment. For the working class, as for the poor, the American Dream and all that sustains it promise a better quality of life. Youth, especially, believe in the promise of employment, vacations, and material possessions. The media and other social institutions uphold these middle-class dreams, but the reality for poor and working-class youth is far from the dream.

Across classes the major life objective for women is marriage. For some the objective is education, work, and marriage. Marriage can be a contradiction for women, for it promises independence but creates dependency. Nevertheless, Chicanas have been socialized to believe that marriage, children, and family are the most valued aspirations. Parental educational aspirations for female children appeared to be at an all-time high in the 1980s, but social structure and family dynamics frequently pushed a young girl into early work responsibilities, pregnancy, and marriage.

Educational pressures plus any one of a variety of dysfunctional coping skills further diminish the life chances of Chicanas. Whereas Anglo middle-income youth engage in sports, hobbies, homework, and dating, Chicano working-class youth are working and/or married. Frequently, young women are in deadend jobs and are homemakers and mothers of one or two babies by the age of eighteen or twenty. Thus while still young they are subjected to the adult stresses of earning an income, paying bills, and raising children.

Because of the national impact of early childrearing, the issue of teen pregnancy is given more attention in Chapter 7. For now it suffices to mention that early childbearing and childrearing set up for most Chicanas a multifaceted cycle of poverty. Because those affected are women, people of color, and generally the poor and working class, or because they come from new middle-class families, they have fewer life chances and are more likely to get trapped in the poverty cycle. Further, the chance of entrapment is greater when the population affected holds the status of the colonized, the conquered, the defeated female.

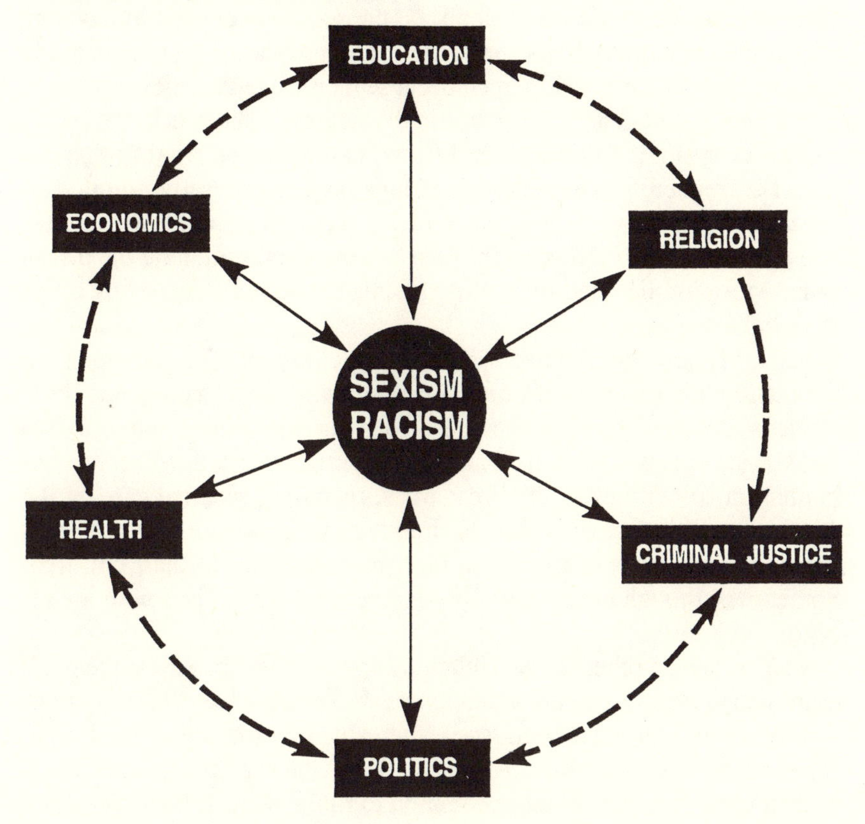

CRIME AND HEALTH

Crime and health are serious Chicana concerns. Each area profoundly affects the Chicana's personal and public life. When these concerns do not specifically touch her life, they at least affect her generally as she deals with the negative stereotype of her people. In part negative characteristics are attributed to her. Because of the negative stereotypes, which depict them as stupid and passive, some Chicanas deny they are Mexican-American.

The Chicana becomes personally involved in male-dominated illegal activities frequently because of her association with men. What this means is that although women retain the power to initiate action or become involved on their own behalf, on the social level women have not yet defined for themselves the written and unwritten rules that guide them. They are governed by men because men make the rules.

It is difficult to make statements on the status of Chicanas in the criminal justice system. Statistics are difficult to obtain, and what can be obtained is frequently contradictory. Chicanas are generally counted as white females. Thus, they remain a hidden population. However, it is known that in the Southwest Chicanas are overrepresented on the prison rolls. Most families find this embarrassing and do not want to talk about it publicly.

Most of these imprisoned women have children. What happens to their children? Perhaps they are on welfare with grandma or some other Chicana female, or perhaps they have been placed in foster homes by social service agents. When they are with other Chicanas, they increase the burden on sometimes limited resources, including medical care. Like other men, Chicanos who see childrearing and childcare as a woman's job rationalize their escape from their responsibility to their children. Sometimes, though not always, these fathers are also in prison or are alcohol and drug addicted.

This brings up other issues: relationships between the sexes; the quality of marriage; divorce and abandonment. Perhaps because opportunities for minorities are limited, some men abandon women and children, while others resort to crime. Although many Chicanas become criminals of their own accord, it is not uncommon to find a woman imprisoned because she was involved with a man who also got convicted; or the woman may be free but engaged in criminal activity because of a man. Likewise, some women who abuse alcohol and drugs or who have AIDS entered the alcohol and drug scene because of a boyfriend, a husband, a relative, or a friend.

Of course, simply to blame Chicano males for female criminal activity, alcoholism, drug use, and AIDS is too simplistic. One must, instead, examine the forces of social, economic, and political control. Who makes the written and unwritten laws, and for whom? Who advertises, and sells alcohol and drugs? Who controls public opinion and the health care system, welfare, social services? Who builds prisons, and for whom? Who monitors prisoners, and why? One has to search widely for areas in which Chicanas and Chicanos really have power, for in reality individual power is highly limited and controlled.

Like criminal statistics, health statistics and health status information are difficult to find. Again, Chicanas are absorbed into the white category. However, it is known, for example, that the number of Chicanas with AIDS is unusually high, as is the number of babies addicted to heroin and/or born with AIDS. In contrast, statistics for breast cancer show the rate is lower among Chicanas than it is among Anglo and black women. Cancer rates are about 25 percent lower among Latinos than among Anglos and blacks in Los Angeles County. The first study of its kind identified striking differences in the incidence and death rates of certain other cancers among this county's diverse racial and ethnic population (*Hispanic Link Weekly Report*, February 13, 1989). For example, the study found the incidence of cervical cancer to be twice as high among Latinas as among Anglo and other non-Hispanic women. For Latinas the number is twenty-one cases per 100,000 women; for Anglos and blacks, eight and fourteen cases respectively per 100,000 women. The breast cancer rate among Latinas, 62 cases per 100,000, is significantly lower than that of Anglo and black women at 106 and 79 cases (respectively) to 100,000 women.

Minimal research on Recombinant 8 syndrome reveals what is typical of medical research on Hispanics. The use of language immediately comes to attention. Ann C. M. Smith, clinical director of genetic services of Children's Hospital in Denver, Colorado (*Rocky Mountain News*, 1982), estimates that at least 500 close and distant relatives of thirty-one known afflicted families stand a chance of transmitting a genetic flaw.

In Recombinant 8 syndrome a relatively rare defect is produced after one of the eighth pair of chromosomes is constructed upside down. Limited research documents families of Hispanic heritage now living in Colorado, New Mexico, and California who have histories of living in a village on the Pecos River in northern New Mexico in the late 1800s. Children of these descendants have a 10 percent chance of receiving an extra, "needless" ration of genetic material in that same flawed, eight-chromosome pair. These children in early infancy often develop holes in their hearts, leaky heart valves, and other serious cardiac flaws. All require open-heart surgery. Those who survive are stunted and severely retarded, move jerkily, and can barely speak. The degrees to which this affects females, both mothers and infants, is not yet known.

Finally, there is the issue of making one's own life: This involves diverse areas like social responsibility, individualism, and competition; it means balancing being a Hispanic female living in Hispanic culture and in Anglo culture; and it includes for the Chicana the struggle against the power and control of men in both cultures. One would think one would go crazy, but Chicanas have not. Some have managed to succeed in all spheres. Others have done well in one or two spheres. Yet others are stalemated in arenas they dislike. The uneven development of women is blatantly evident. This, of course, flies in the face of those who desire simplistic lives and attempt to stereotype Chicanas. This also raises the issue of the need for more research, applied research that addresses or attempts to solve Chicana concerns.

REFERENCES

Elsasser, Nan, Kyle MacKenzie, and Yvonne Tixier y Vigil. 1980. *Las Mujeres: Conversations from a Hispanic Community*. New York: Feminist Press.

Garcia, Christina. 1988. "Shake Your Body." In *Time* (July 11): 50-52.

Garcia, John. 1983. "Chicano Political Development: Examining Participation in the Decade of Hispanics." National Chicano Council of Higher Education, *La Red/The Network*, 72 (September, 1983): 9.

Hispanic Link Weekly Report. 1989. Vol. 7, No. 8 (February 20): 2.

______. 1988. Vol. 7, No. 7 (February 13): 2.

Hughes, Robert. 1988. "Magnifico! Hispanic Culture Breaks Out of the Barrio." In *Time* (July 11): 50-52.

Lacayo, Richard. 1988. "A Surging New Spirit." In "Magnifico! Hispanic Culture Breaks Out of the Barrio." *Time* (July 11): 46-49. This article was reported by Scott Brown, Christina Garcia, and Edward M. Gomez.

Perez, Emma. 1991. "Sexuality and Discourse: Notes from a Chicana Survivor," in Carla Trujillo, *Chicana Lesbianis: The Girls Our Mothers Warned Us About*. Berkeley: Third Woman Press, 169.

Rocky Mountain News. 1982. "Flawed Gene." (August 31): 10.

Sierra, Christine M. 1988. "Chicano Politics after 1984." In Juan R. Garcia, Julia Curry Rodriguez, and Clara Lomas, eds., *Times of Challenge: Chicanos and Chicanas in American Society*. Houston: University of Houston Press, Monograph Series No. 6. 7-24.

Chapter 6

Elderly Chicanas

It has been said that aging is the great equalizer. Is it? Some older people suffer more than others, enduring more hardships throughout their lives and as they grow old. Yet other elderly are quite comfortable in their old age, perhaps because they have been comfortable all their lives. They experience relatively little change in status, while other elderly experience considerable change. Thus, contemporary elderly people are a highly diverse group. They differ in income, health, and social support networks as well as by gender and race (ethnicity). They also differ in how they are affected by national policy.

The elderly do, however, have one thing in common: being elderly. Some people in the United States can escape racism, some can escape sexism, but not many can escape aging and the discrimination attached to it. This chapter reviews the status of Mexican-American females in gerontological research. It also reviews their nature and character, with special emphasis upon their gender and cultural roles.

A SOCIOLOGICAL CONCEPT OF AGING

Social science study of the elderly Hispanic has primarily focused upon whether race or ethnicity would increase or decrease eligibility and accessibility to social services. This research focus has led to the understanding of the senior Chicanos in terms of those things held in common with all elderly, but it also has articulated those things held in common with other Chicano people.

Many factors shape the human experience. It is in the study of the elderly Chicana that one gains significant insight into the role ethnicity plays in the life of Mexican-Americans. Some factors to be considered in the study of ethnicity are gender, country of origin, socioeconomic status, lifespan or longevity, life chances, color, and the ethnic support network. Preliminary findings reveal that honor and respect, family and children, and the environment, community, and language are important factors for the population, factors that surface in studies on youth and middle-aged Chicanos and that define values and direct the quality of life among the Chicano elderly.

A discussion attached to the quality of life for aging Americans is: What constitutes aging? For many people aging is simple. One birthday follows another. Social scientists do not view aging so simplistically. They see a relationship between chronological age and the social expectations, roles, norms, and perceptions attached to that age. This relationship is also culturally relevant.

Unlike in dominant America, in Mexican-American culture social influence increases with age. Seniors are the authorities on the subjects of values, norms, and culture. What the dominant culture maintains about elderly people does not matter. In spite of great social pressure, Chicanos have not adhered to a diminished role for seniors.

In the Chicano experience, seniors lend direction to the future by means of the socialization of children, counseling of adults, recounting of history, and transfer of knowledge. However, as the general Chicano population becomes more urbanized and internalizes more Anglo values, there is a threat to the Chicano elderly of relegating the elder's expertise to an area of folklore, an area that to some extent lacks legitimacy. This results in the alienation of seniors and their displacement from full participation in the life of the community.

Attention to the older minority person has been significant, although limited to infrequent reports and articles. In 1970 the U.S. Bureau of the Census reported that Native Americans and Mexican-Americans had a life expectancy of less than sixty years. In 1980 the American Association of Retired Persons (AARP) estimated that the life expectancy for Mexican-Americans was higher, especially for women.

In 1971 the White House Conference on Aging gave special attention to the needs and circumstances of aging minority people. At this conference, common concern for a nonchronological definition of aging was voiced Many believed the conventional chronological definition, while convenient, inherently discriminated against minority elderly because socially and mentally they aged faster than the majority elderly population. This accelerated mental or intellectual aging, it was felt, was a result of the impact of various institutional variables over which racial and ethnic minorities had little control.

Besides the concept of chronological aging is the theory of functional age: the contention that individuals age at different rates and that an estimate of an individual's age has dimensions that are mentally constructed. In layperson's terms, some people mature faster than others because of the way they think or what they believe. I would like to add that some people are seen as older because of the way the social scientists studying them think and what they believe. In the case of the Chicano, for example, because Chicanos endure more social stresses, many social scientists think Chicanos age faster.

AGING AND THE REALITY FACTOR

Hispanics do not age faster. They only appear aged. They have wisdom and sophistication about the realities of life because they are not trapped into the dominant lifestyle that defines them. They have experience and can more easily see the structure and function of various social forces. Older Chicanas know racism and sexism through their experience. Enduring certain truths tires them, beats them down. Certain symbols are associated with aging: drab-colored skin, wrinkles, depression, poverty, illness. In addition, the elderly are often stereotyped as wards of the state, as welfare cases. One thus visualizes the aged without recognizing that what one sees are the effects of social institutional forces that bestow upon Mexican-Americans, in particular, a difficult life.

Aging requires an integration of much knowledge and an acceptance of reality. For Chicanos this means integrating and accepting the knowledge and realities of living in two cultures, two social systems that have systematically been in conflict. This can result in the stereotyped symbols of aging, but it also can stimulate creative mental activity. No exam has measured how the elderly deal with the conflicts, how they balance the two systems. Existing measurement instruments and theories are inadequate. Perhaps the closest related research has been conducted in the area of social aging.

Social age uses functional age as a base to identify psychological variables in its measurement. Some factors considered are abilities, personality, and self-concept. An integration or synthesis of the two concepts and the emergence of social-psychological definition might be the most productive. A new definition would bring immediate relief to minorities.

This would immediately affect the retirement and eligibility age for social security.

Almost forty years ago age sixty-five was arbitrarily set as the retirement age. This age has hurt in particular those who are stronger and do not want to retire. The system has worked against the Chicano population because some Chicanos have the needs of elderly people at a much earlier age. Of course, they can receive other social services and become wards of the state at an earlier age.

Receipt of such benefits, especially social security, displays racial (ethnic) disparities. For example, more Chicanos than Anglos depend on social security benefits as their only source of income, but more Anglos than Chicanos receive social security benefits. Many Chicanos cannot obtain "insured status" because so many of their employers did not properly report all earnings. In addition, racial discrimination in employment and lower earnings result in lower benefits, and many minority seniors do not apply for other income-support benefits such as supplemental security income because they do not know that it exists, or because they are reluctant to interact with intimidating bureaucracies. How these services are administered has also given the Chicano elderly the perception that Anglo service providers do not respect them.

Finally, some individuals are unsure of their resident status or are in the country without documentation and thus fear deportation. They do not apply for social security and other social services because certification of citizenship is required and they do not possess such proof. Some lack birth certificates because they were born at home or in small villages, and so their birth was never recorded. Others went to school when a birth record was not required, or they went to school in an area where the policy was not enforced. They have never voted, and may not know how to drive. Some of these people do not read and frequently depend on those who can to assist them.

Social security is a concern for all elderly people, including Chicanas. Now that more women and more minorities have higher incomes and stand to collect better benefits, there is an apparent threat to the national social security fund. All this, of course, is due to changing demographics and fundamental decisions at the federal level about the course of national policy. Social services to the elderly have not been a priority. The threat to social security includes the physical security of individuals and the threat of war in Central and Latin America, and women have not played a role in making these decisions. These policies have been made by white males.

Many of these policy makers are older white men who are part of a network generally referred to as the "old boys' club." As the older men die off or retire, they pass on the decision-making power to other white males of their same mentality. Many minorities and women feel that, were they in power, they would define a different national priority, another lifestyle. Some have thought that coalitions are a strengthening strategy. Women, especially black and Hispanic women, were the first coalition builders to address political and economic issues of concern to racial (ethnic) minorities and females of all ages.

CONTINUITY IN LIFE EXPERIENCES

Elderly Chicanos tend to use natural networks to communicate. When information is needed, the elder questions family, friends, neighbors, or other trusted individuals, who also feel free to give the senior suggestions. Assisting Chicano elders usually means more than sharing information. It means being with the individuals physically, helping them help themselves, linking them up with another trusted individual within the network, or referring and introducing the elders to someone trusted who knows another trusted person (Vale, 1977). Although this mode of operation may be seen by the outsider as dependency, it is not. It is a communal, cultural means of obtaining information and securing services, social contact, and nurturing.

Most of us believe that when people get old, they stop changing and contributing to society. However, growth and change and contributions do continue throughout life, with each phase of life having its own characteristics, adaptations, and limitations (Facio, 1985; Levinson, 1978; Sheehy, 1978; Gould, 1972). In Chicano culture the elderly are often called upon to discuss the history of social and personal change and what has shaped society. They are the repositories of cultural wisdom. They give guidance in problem solving and child rearing.

Generally, the gerontological focus by traditional social scientists on Mexican-Americans is weak. It fails to articulate what takes place in the continuity of the elderly Chicanos' life experience, but it does reveal the special needs of older Chicanas. Some research insinuates that the population is a problem. This is more directly linked to the emphasis on youth in this country: People tend to view aging as a problem. The perception is also linked to the expectation that elderly Chicanas have more economic and health problems than other women their age. Lacking in research emphasis is what the elderly Chicana contributes to the continuity of life: to her family, her community, and her society.

DIVERSITY AND DEMOGRAPHICS

Ramón Vale (1983) estimated that older Hispanics comprised 4.5 percent of the total Hispanic population. Vale notes that there are problems with estimating the number of Hispanic elderly because there is a problem with estimating the number of Hispanics. Estimates on the number of Hispanics range from 5 million to 120 million. This demographic inconsistency is due to the large number of undocumented immigrants who do not report their presence in the United States.

Elderly Hispanics come from various countries: Mexico, Puerto Rico, Cuba, Central America, and Latin America, as well as the United States. According to the AARP (1987) nearly 673,000 (about 5 percent) of the Hispanic population are sixty-five years of age or over; of those, almost 45,000 (6.6 percent) are eighty-five years of age or older.

The AARP also estimates that among Hispanics aged sixty to sixty-four, there are eighty-six men for every one hundred women. The sex ratio declines with age, however: sixty-one men for every one hundred women at age eighty-five. (See table.) Eleven percent live in rural areas. This is less than half that of rural white elderly (26 percent). Thus, like the general Chicano population, older Hispanics tend to live in cities.

Most U.S. Hispanics live in the four states of California, Texas, Florida, and New York. California and Texas have a high Mexican population, while Florida has a high concentration of Cubans and New York a high concentration of Puerto Ricans and persons from the Caribbean Islands.

EDUCATION, INCOME, AND EMPLOYMENT

A review of the literature quickly reveals an interest in the rapidly rising number of Chicano seniors. It also quickly reveals they are poorer and less educated than older Anglos. Because of language differences and cultural practices, Hispanic elderly are more susceptible to consumer abuse; they also suffer significantly from class, age, and racial discrimination. Women are faced with the additional victimization of sexism. Thus, generally, the Chicano experience is exacerbated by old age. Seniors are more dependent on public benefits, but they may be the least likely to obtain social benefits. Often they may also not live long enough to receive full social benefits (Gelford, 1982).

Of all minority elderly, those of Hispanic background are, indeed, least educated. The proportion with no formal schooling is eight times as great as for Anglos (AARP, 1980). Of Hispanics sixty-five years

Gender Ratio by Race and Ethnicity (males per 100 females)

Race or Ethnicity	AGE				
+85	60 - 64	65 - 69	70 - 74	75 - 79	80 - 84
Anglo 43	87	81	72	61	52
Black 50	80	73	69	63	60
Hispanic 61	86	76	77	76	73
Asian Pacific Islander 60	84	93	109	89	67
Native American 59	87	77	82	74	66

Source: "A Portrait of Older Minorities," The American Association of Minority Affairs Initiative. American Association of Retired Persons (AARP), based on the 1980 Census of Population, U.S. Department of Commerce, Bureau of the Census, Washington, D.C.

and older,16 percent have had no education and only 19 percent graduated from high school. These statistics are significant, since education is closely linked to employment in the United States. The percentage of Hispanic elderly in the labor force is the same as that in the Anglo population, 13 percent. Yet the percentage of unemployed workers is nearly twice as great among elderly Hispanics (9 percent) as among Anglos (5 percent).

Perhaps the 1990 census will give us more current statistics, but in 1980 the median personal income of men aged sixty-five years or more was $4,592, or 62 percent that of Anglo males the same age. Elderly Hispanic women had a median income of $2,873, while Anglo elderly women had a median income of $3,894. The percentage of Hispanic elderly with incomes below the poverty level was twice as large (26 percent) as among elderly Anglos (13 percent). Poverty rates were higher in rural than in urban areas and higher among women than men. Thus, rural women were the most impoverished group of all. For example, among the Hispanic elderly, 38 percent of rural women have a below-poverty income as compared to 21 percent of Anglo rural women. Statistics are not expected to be very different in the near future.

ELDERLY CHICANA LIFE EXPERIENCES

Linda Facio (1985) contends that life experiences differ by gender, race, ethnicity, and class. She notes that, on the whole, not only are elderly women poorer than elderly men, but they tend to live longer and tend to live alone. She cites a lack of information on the experiences of elderly Chicanas but notes that this is due to the highly fragmented and inconclusive status of gerontological research.

The lack of this information is remedied a bit by the AARP, which asserts that nearly twice as many Hispanic men as women age sixty and older are married and living with their spouses. This is consistent with a pattern mirrored in the Anglo elderly population. A finding in need of more research is that almost twice as many older Hispanic men and women as Anglos are divorced or separated. The same proportion of Hispanic women and Anglo women are widowed.

Michael Gilfix asserts that poverty is without a doubt the leading factor creating visible differences between all minority seniors and Anglo seniors (1977). Whereas Anglos become poor in their old age, Chicanos suffer a far less perceptible decline in income. This is because elderly Hispanics have always been poorer than Anglos. It is the drop in Anglo income that makes it appear that Chicanos suffer a far less perceptible decline in income. In addition, there might be a matter of differential perception. Older Chicanos might not see themselves as poorer because they measure wealth differently. They place more emphasis on the social quality of their lives than they do on the material aspects. Social relationships, health (not always linked to money for Chicanos), and company in their old age are of primary concern. The student of Chicano elderly should not be confused; money is also recognized as an important necessity, but its value is secondary.

It is in this aspect of aging that, Facio maintains, the Chicana has an advantage. There appears to be more continuity for older Mexican women than there is for men. In their old age men have to make a change from predominantly public lives—the life outside of the home—to private life, within the realm of the home and family. Aging Anglos make the same change, but not with the same emotional tone. Chicanos, for the most part, value home and family more. Thus, elderly Hispanic men experience more continuity than do Anglo males.

VALUES, HEALTH, AND HOUSING

Bryan Kemp, a University of Southern California clinical associate professor, and Kenneth Brummel-Smith, also an associate professor, but of the family medicine's geriatrics section, got elderly people to cooperate with their study of depression among Hispanic elderly. They documented that elderly Hispanics in southern California have a high rate of depression symptoms and receive very little mental health treatment in mental health centers (1989).

Their data also suggest that older Hispanics are at least as likely as non-Hispanics of the same age to visit a general medical doctor for treatment of symptoms related to depression. Medical treatment often reflects psychological problems in the form of physical ailments. A primary physician may be called upon if a patient has a stomachache. Most physicians immediately prescribe medication to address the symptom, not the problem, therefore not curing the patient.

Kemp and Brummel-Smith maintain that elderly Hispanics are less likely to talk about their physical symptoms, which may include sleeplessness, lack of energy, and loss of appetite. They warn, however, that these statements should be considered with caution. Kemp and Brummel-Smith do not warn that Hispanic elderly may be less likely to talk about their physical symptoms to Anglos only.

The southern California study provides no explanation of the high rate of depression among elderly Hispanics, but it shows correlations with several risk factors for depression, one of the leading mental health ailments in the nation (Gelman, 1987). Among these factors are low income, medical disabilities, low level of education, isolation, having family members who have health problems, and impaired mobility.

A factor that may affect Hispanics specifically is language. This along with the factors mentioned keeps the elderly person out of the mainstream of social activities and perhaps without as much formal socia support. "Formal social support" is not operationally or situationally defined by Kemp and Brummel-Smith. Hispanic elderly, especially women, have some social support systems within their culture, family, and neighborhood, but they have few support systems in the dominant society.

Information on elderly Hispanic health is provided by the AARP. It reports that of all groups sixty-five and over living in the community, not in nursing homes, 85 percent reported having at least one chronic ailment. Forty-five percent report some limitation in performing day-to-day activities. The Hispanic elderly have somewhat higher rates of activity limitation (48 percent) and have more days per year in bed because of illness.

Not only are Chicano elders less healthy, they are also less affluent than Anglo elderly. They live in low-quality housing. The AARP estimates that about 97 percent live in households in the community alone, with family members, or with nonrelatives. The remainder (3 percent) generally live in nursing homes. However, among the elderly eighty-five or older, only 10 percent of Hispanics are in nursing homes as compared to 23 percent of Anglos. Seventy-two percent of Hispanic elderly live with at least one family member, a slightly higher percentage than the white elderly (69 percent).

RESEARCH AND CULTURAL CONTINUITY

In studying the elderly Mexican-American, Deborah Newquist (1977) discovered that conducting research in minority communities uncovered some ethical and cultural questions that traditional social scientists have not encountered before and that they have failed to address. Foremost among these was the ethics of having the social scientist bring something of value to the community, not to the informant, in return for valuable information or participation in a study.

It is not surprising that this would be discovered working among the aged. Again, it is in old age that one finds salient cultural indicators in the Chicano community. Chicano researchers and community members view social science research ethics and accountability differently than do Anglos. Reciprocity, exchange, not necessarily monetary in nature, is highly valued. It is the usual cultural expectation.

In Chicano culture one gives, not repays, a visit with a visit, a kindness with a kindness. Younger people are expected to defer to adults, particularly to seniors, especially women. Social science academics of the dominant culture do not engage in such exchange or in such deference. They prefer to use an ivory-tower approach to their study of the minority community. Knowing this, the community distrusts researchers, for they require information but do not give anything in return, as Chicano culture would demand. As long as researchers remain insensitive, Chicanos will tell them what they want to hear. They will continue to give false information. Indeed, many choose not to cooperate at all.

Some misleading conclusions have been made about the elderly, conclusions that affect the study of Chicanos and Chicanas in general. A commonly held stereotype is that the elderly are firmly supported by their strong nuclear families and their extended family networks. Newquist (1977) found this true in a specialized way: The family is definitely a resource in terms of social and emotional support; but because of its social and historical experience, it tends not to be a strong service provider. This statement, however, should not be misinterpreted to mean the family will not help. Rather, the family also lacks resources, but helps as much as their resources allow.

Newquist found that older Chicanos do not expect as much from their families as the study anticipated. In fact, they expect even less than do older Anglos. Newquist's work also documented that a lifetime of discrimination and survival has made minorities more adaptive, resourceful, and able to cope. This is a highly sophisticated, realistic group of people. They do not expect as much as Anglos because they know their families also suffer the effects of social discrimination and limited opportunities.

Very specific coping mechanisms exist among the entire Chicano population, especially among elderly women who have had to contend with various social forces simultaneously. An area deserving study is the role of ethnicity as a coping mechanism, and how it acts as a source of continuity. Ethnicity as a continuity factor is especially important in light of the fact that minorities in the United States experience so much social change and crisis because of their minority status. Under these circumstances, the one thing that remains constant for Chicanos is the nourishment of their rich culture. This is significant, particularly in light of the importance of continuity of life patterns in the well-being of the total person. Cultural background certainly lends the elder Chicano strength and support.

REFERENCES

American Association of Retired Persons (AARP). 1987. "Portrait of Older Minorities." Washington, D.C.

Facio, Elisa, "Linda." 1985. "Gender and Aging: A Case Study of Mexican/Chicana Elderly." *Trabajos Monográficos: Studies in Chicana/Latina Research*, Vol. 1, No. 1: 5-21.

Gelford, Donald. 1982. "Aging: The Ethnic Factor." Boston: Little, Brown.

Gelman, David. 1987. "Depression." *Newsweek* (May 4): 48-57.

Gilfix, Michael. 1977. "A Case of Unequal Suffering." *Generations 3*. Western Gerontological Society. Summer: 8-11.

Gould, Roger. 1972a. *Transformations*. New York: Simon & Schuster.

______. 1972b. "The Phases of Adult Life: A Study of Developmental Psychology." *American Journal of Psychiatry*, Vol. 129, No. 5: 521-31.

Kemp, Bryan, and Kenneth Brummel-Smith. 1989. "Depression in Elderly Hispanics Often Goes Untreated." *La Voz Hispana de Colorado*, XVL (January 25): 5.

Levinson, Daniel. 1978. *Seasons of a Man's Life*. New York: Ballantine Books.

Miranda, M., and R. Ruiz. 1983. "The Demography of Mexican-American Aging." In M. Miranda and R. Ruiz, eds., *Chicano Aging and Mental Health*. Rockville, Md.: National Institute of Mental Health. 8-16.

Newquist, Deborah. 1977. "Aging across Cultures." *Generations*. Western Geronto-logical Society. Summer: 8-13.

Sheehy, Gail. 1978. *Passages*. New York: Bantam Books.

Vale, Ramón. 1977. "Natural Networks: Paths to Service." *Generations*. Western Gerontological Society. Summer: 36-44.

Chapter 7

Cultural Synthesis: Breaking Barriers and Defining New Roles

This chapter reviews how La Chicana balances two strong cultures. While doing so, she has broken old barriers to reach nontraditional goals and has, in turn, encountered new barriers and new goals. She has balanced defining new roles while maintaining old cultural traditions and building new ones. This chapter not only analyzes cultural synthesis, it also explores the impact of this new development on men in particular and society in general. If studied carefully, the Chicana experience has the potential to guide Anglo, male-dominated society in values clarification and redefinition.

POVERTY AND THE SINGLE FEMALE HEAD OF HOUSEHOLD

Single female heads of household, regardless of ethnicity or race, share a particular characteristic in that they tend to be poor; however, the feminization of poverty is more characteristic of women of color than it is of Anglo women. Because of the social forces of triple discrimination (race, class, and gender) brought to bear against Chicanas, and because of resulting limited opportunities and individual actions such as making bad choices, many of them are poor. The nature of poverty and the poverty cycle is well researched. However, not much is known about the nature and character of the women who have broken the cycle and emerged into a new lifestyle.

The topic of single parenting by women gives rise to such issues as raising children alone, the single mother's relationships with men, and the effect of the single-parent lifestyle on the family. Sometimes for single mothers these issues are complicated by other concerns. For some women immigrant status makes life more complex. For these and other poor women, health care is another concern. Some single mothers in poverty have concerns that go beyond immigrant status and health care: They worry about the war and warlike conditions created by men in Central and Latin America, where they have left behind family and friends. The male-dominated U.S. government, of course, is heavily involved in these areas.

When poverty is not an issue the image is. The media promotes stereotyping that supports discrimination. Marketing firms and large corporations have discovered the substantial purchasing power of the population and are now targeting it. Hispanic women are not a concern by themselves, but when they are put into larger categories of populations with "new money," minorities, and women, marketing departments get interested. The quality and potential danger of some advertised products aimed at the minority market remain an issue, of course. The earliest attempts to market to these populations were from the cigarette and alcohol industries, for example. Although the power wielded by the advertising industry—in creating images and enticing buyers—has been of limited concern to Chicana feminists, it is a force to be reckoned with by all upwardly mobile feminists as well as the minority poor.

One might ask: What does marketing have to do with poverty and immigrant women? The point is that Chicanas can fall into the trap of what the media sets up as the ideal lifestyle: one that promotes materialism so that the individual will consume more and more goods. This is contrary to the traditional Chicana value system, which emphasizes community. If a Chicana inadvertently adopts this individualist lifestyle, she risks alienation from her own people, yet she will not be totally accepted by the dominant group. At the same time one must not accept that poverty is a cultural variable, for it is defined and imposed from outside the culture. The task for most Chicanas is how to break the poverty cycle, emerge into a new lifestyle, yet remain true to one's self.

SOCIAL CHANGE AND CULTURAL BLENDING

Traditional Chicana culture has defined success as consisting of respect, good health, having family, and valuing human beings regardless of age, gender, or race. As Chicanas endure economic social stress, urbanization, the women's movement, the impact of the media, the Chicano movement, and so on, their values change. Income, urbanization, experience, education—all influence ideology, the set of ideas used to justify and defend the interests and actions of a group. The shared knowledge and its ideological basis we call culture guide the values, norms, and roles of men and women. Thus, as their ideology is affected, the Chicanas' cultural outlook changes.

Language plays a large part in cultural change. The structure of culture is frequently consistent with the structure of language; take away the language, and the structure of the culture becomes vulnerable and easy to change. Many contemporary Chicanas do not speak Spanish. Yet they have been socialized in Mexican-American culture and are culturally Chicano. To illustrate the importance of language, it is important to note that the word *Chicana* is an ideological term denoting a certain way of thinking, acting, and believing. Prior to the 1960s this term had negative connotations. This is no longer true. Stereotypes of a Chicana have caused some women to become embarrassed and alienated from its contemporary positive meaning and to reject the label.

In dominant-subordinate relationships the stripping and demeaning of language is important as a means of maintaining social control over the Chicano population. For example, it strips people who use the Spanish language of giving direction to their specific ways, values, norms, and roles: what they believe, how and where they do things. As mentioned, individuals can be of Chicano culture without speaking Spanish. They learn what is important, how and where to do certain things, in the Spanish-based Chicano tradition. Thus, what they do is Chicano in origin, but they enact it in English.

As Chicanas interact with more dominant Americans, they learn and even internalize Anglo values, language norms, and roles. Social institutions promote this internalization of Anglo values at the same time that Chicano values are deemed unworthy, unscientific, old-fashioned, or impractical. But there is resistance to Chicano culture becoming too strongly influenced by Anglo characteristics. As cultural exchange and internalization increase, Chicanas risk becoming more individualistic and less communal, more profit oriented, more competitive, and less willing to share what they have attained. These new behaviors and attitudes can become dominant, they can be resisted, or they can be tempered to exist in balance with Chicano culture. Some Chicanas choose to change cultures, while others choose to be bicultural.

Cultural blending or being bicultural manifests itself among Chicanas in some highly specific ways. Most Chicanas share some cultural values with some Anglo women, for example, concern for relationship to the environment. Chicanas tend to believe that people should live in harmony with the environment, not in opposition to it. Likewise, some Anglo women are concerned about preserving the natural environment and living in harmony with nature. Another important example is that they share the need to empower women, thereby influencing change in the current social structure that frequently discriminates against both groups.

CHANGING GENDER ROLES AND THEIR IMPACT UPON CULTURE

When La Chicana ventures out of her prescribed role, Chicano men react in much the same way as Anglo men react to Anglo women when they find themselves in the same situation. They can be supportive or resistant. They may adapt, or they may leave women for ones more to their liking. Resistance may be blatant or passive. Frequently the Anglo feminist counterreaction is to create distance from men. Chicanas are not as quick to create distance from their men as are some Anglo feminists. Unity is more important to Chicano social existence. Chicana resistance to creating distance finds some of its base in the Chicano public school experience. Both Chicanas and Chicanos tend to have had their first negative experience with Anglo female teachers and principals in the American educational system. Because young people spend so much time in school, these experiences have been intense. Chicanos know Anglo females are socialized in a society that practices racism, and therefore tend to distrust these women. Chicanos also believe that Anglo women have a tendency to be more individualistic and competitive and to have a higher profit orientation than do Chicano males and females. Chicanos want more than this taught to their children. Many Chicano people do not want to contribute to this racist, profit-motivated mentality, or to break up the unity of the Chicano civil rights movement on issues that strongly impact the community.

The production of individuals who think and act like dominant Anglos is a devastating thought to those who have dedicated twenty to thirty years to the Chicano civil rights movement. In the community a Chicana or Chicano who has internalized Anglo values and norms is a "coconut," that is, a brown Anglo, or a Chicano with brown skin and a white mentality. The black community makes a similar designation: An "oreo" is a person who is black but thinks white.

A DELICATE BALANCE

As Chicanas gain upward mobility, they also must shoulder a delicate balance. The first area in which Chicanas deviate from traditional roles is in the area of work outside the home. If the Chicana goes to work, grandma or another female generally provides inexpensive daycare. This may limit Chicanas to childcare and trap them into low-paying positions with limited lateral or upward mobility, and it certainly sets up an exploitative relationship. There can, however, be another perspective. The need for daycare may weave older women more firmly into the social fabric of the dominant society, as well as into the Chicano family and social structure. Since daycare is of primary importance to women, it may create new opportunities for Chicanas.

As Chicanas gain access to information, they gain social power. And as they gain social power, the old cultural structures change. (See figure.)

Cultural Change Pattern

Access to Information⟶Social Power⟶Cultural Change⟶Access to Information

As Chicanas gain information, they are able to change their lives. For example, Chicanas now know they no longer have to remain in uncomfortable, negative, or abusive relationships. Frequently, leaving the situation or even divorce is the answer. However, there appears a cultural lag between what women know and what they do. Not all women leave or demand change in their uncomfortable, negative, or abusive relationships. The reasons they remain are varied and individual. Women may remain in these relationships because they are economically dependent. For the Chicana social dependency is also a factor. The value of family is paramount, and what the community will say is highly regarded.

CHICANO MALE-GENDER ROLES

Men have always felt freer to abandon children and women, thereby contributing to the feminization of poverty. Children now live among the poorest conditions in the nation. Part of the problem is that women and children in American society lack worth. Female-headed households are alternative family structures highly represented in Chicano culture. This family form is severely disdained and socially punished: The punishment for having been abandoned by a man, for having left a destructive relationship, is poverty.

As Chicano men have internalized more Anglo male values, their sexism manifests itself in numerous ways. Society has denied Chicano males its symbols of human worth: power, money, and control of resources. The human need for power forces the Chicano to exert power where he can. Because most vehicles of power are denied him, because they are culturally foreign to Chicanos, he exerts power over the lives of women, for women are an available, easy target to control. Chicanos and Chicanas need to recognize male exertion of power over women as the oppression of sexism and racism and take steps to stop abusive cycles. Men and women with self-esteem, love of one another, and a high value for family do not enter or sustain abusive relationships.

Because the dominant society so highly values high income among men, an increase in female earning power cuts into perceived male social power and worth. Among some Chicanas there is a fear that what has happened to some black males might also happen to Chicano men: The discrimination process has worked to emasculate many black men by depriving them of earning power, the established criterion by which manhood is bestowed. This process has resulted in depriving them of power and human worth and resources. Minority women and men need to recognize this as the manipulation of sexism and racism and enter into an alliance whereby both become empowered. Thus, it is in the Chicano male's interest to enter into feminist dialogue with Chicanas. But how?

One solution is to change the criterion for success, or what makes a human being worthy. The Chicano definition of success (having respect, good health, and family) has been discussed. Being rich or economically comfortable is now the criterion for success in the United States. But what about the old-fashioned notion that humans have worth because they are human and alive? Must people be productive to be valued? Production, especially production for profit, of course, is a modern Anglo value attached to all humans. More and more, success is measured by accumulated resources, the result of production.

CLOSING THE DECADE OF THE HISPANIC

The theme of the 1987 National Association of Chicano Studies conference in Salt Lake City, Utah, was "Can Chicanos Survive Their Decade?" Despite a hint of doubt at the time, the general feeling was that because of their increasing social and political power, unlike ever before Hispanics were in a position to make an impact not only upon their own culture but upon society in general. Three years later that general feeling of 1987 had grown to great enthusiasm in the Chicano community, when planning for the year 2000 was the theme in many upward-mobility workshops, conferences, and public presentations.

The enthusiasm in planning for the year 2000 can be attributed to new-found motivation based on demographics and the fact that Hispanics are the nation's largest ethnic population group. In addition, the Reagan administration had come to an end, and Hispanics felt that with President Bush there could be some negotiation as the population attempted to recover from the severe setbacks of the Reagan years in social programs which had benefited minorities. During the Reagan administration Chicanos were negatively affected by changes in programs for the aging, health, education, and legal aid.

Hispanics outlined their issues. The list hardly looked any different from the list of the 1960s, but some of the language was different. Foremost among the issues listed was economic development. Poverty was included on the economic development list, but the late 1980s list had a definite working- and middle-class flavor. Economic development meant jobs for people but it also meant investing in the community to better the quality of life in poor Chicano neighborhoods. The issues of poverty were part of the language because so many Chicanos were poor. Many Chicanos (both middle-income and poor) worked on these issues; but somehow the issues of poverty were overshadowed by working-class and middle-income issues. The explanation for this, of course, was that the working and middle classes had suffered severe blows under the Reagan Republican administration. Unions had been busted and many Chicanos plunged deeper into the poverty ranks. The middle-income group, which consisted primarily of professionals, clung to what it had acquired during the last twenty years and struggled to obtain more.

Except for academia and Chicana support for research on Chicanas, during this time there was little movement in feminist circles. Anglo women struggled to maintain what little was left of feminist support networks and services. The Reagan years had been hard on them also. Men, especially white men, were definitely in control.

In the mid- to late 1980s the lack of women in leadership again became a Chicana issue (it had been an issue in the 1960s), especially at a conference on educational and economic development in Denver, Colorado, early in 1989. Because there were no women on the program, the women at that conference decided to hold their own conference to talk about gender discrimination by Hispanic men.

But generally other discussions and actions focused upon women in business and the building of leadership in corporations. Although poor women were an issue, the emphasis was on working and professional women. In the general community boycotting the Coors Corporation of Golden, Colorado, was still an issue. The corporation had endured the twenty-year boycott of its beer and was trying desperately to make amends and increase its profit margin, especially in the Chicano community. It heavily funded Chicano functions, and it poured money into leadership development seminars for Hispanic women.

The controversy over Coors continued. Many women agreed with men that the boycott should be honored and that women should not take money from Coors. Some women felt it was all right to take the money but not drink the beer. Yet others felt that if they accepted the money, they should buy the beer.

This was only one of the issues that fragmented the Chicana community. Jealousy and alienation among women was frequent. First apparent in middle schools and high schools, it is also obvious in the professional world, where Chicanas strive for upward mobility within the corporate structure. They wear business suits, attend meetings with men, and talk about mentoring other women but never have the time to do so. One thing is sure: Chicanas have worked hard in the professional world and, even though they have not achieved success as frequently and in the numbers that Anglo women have, they have done well within the corporate structure.

LATINAS IN THE CORPORATE STRUCTURE

Company officials at Avon Corporation believed there was a problem in conducting direct sales within the inner city, and therefore did not pursue a metropolitan market. Laura Estrada and other Latinas helped them break into that market. Another inner-city corporation, Princess House, which specializes in selling crystal products, has experienced great success thanks to the efforts of Lillian Melgar and many Hispanic professional women. In 1987 Melgar supervised 700 members of a mostly Latina sales force and sold more than $5 million worth of products in the Los Angeles area.

Attesting to the Latina's contributions and success is Charito Kruvant. In 1988 Kruvant, president of Creative Associates, which she had founded twelve years earlier, was one of the recipients of the Women of Enterprise Awards given by the Small Business Association and Avon Corporation. She and many other women are examples of Latinas venturing into the predominantly Anglo and male field of business.

Hispanic businesses have been growing rapidly (*Hispanic*, 1988). Although there are few Latinas in business, they do comprise some of the leadership. Mercedes Olivera (Vista, 1989) notes that according to federal reports, women became the fastest-growing segment of the business community in the late 1970s. Presently 3.7 million female-owned businesses exist in the nation. This number is growing at about one and one-half times the rate of male-owned businesses. About 28 percent of this total figure consists of female sole proprietorships.

However, all is not well for women in business. Only 2 percent of America's top management posts are held by women (Olivera, 1989). Furthermore, when women are represented in top management, they tend to earn substantially less than their male peers.

Like their Anglo counterparts, an increasing number of Hispanic women are turning to entrepreneurship. Hispanic female entrepreneurs share with Anglo entrepreneurs similar reasons for starting their own business. They want more pay. They have great ideas. They also tend to share common personal traits with the average male entrepreneur. They are innovators, they are independent, and they are risk takers. A current study for the Small Business Association and the Minority Business Development Agency shows that more than half (54 percent) of Hispanic women business owners are in home-based businesses (Olivera, 1989). The main attraction is that a home-based business enables them to reconcile family demands and career pressures.

As Chicanas become entrepreneurs, they confront numerous problems. One is changing from team player to team leader. Another, and perhaps the biggest, problem women have in beginning their own businesses is access to venture capital. For example, it took Gloria Del Carmen Rodriguez, publisher of *Hispanic Entrepreneur*, of New York, a year to obtain venture capital for her magazine. She advises women to avoid banks, and to approach venture capital and investment firms for financing. Yet other problems women have in beginning businesses is disorganization, a reluctance to delegate responsibility, and a lack of sophistication in dealing with the old boys' network. As Margarita Poza, coowner of Publix Insurance Agency in Florida, reports, men admire a woman's "spunkiness" as long as it is not directed at them.

Olivera (1989) notes that women must reconcile four contradictory sets of expectations when starting their own business: (1) They have to take risks, but be consistently outstanding in their field. (2) They have to be tough, but not macho. (3) They must be ambitious, but not expect equal treatment. (4) They must take responsibility, but be willing to follow others' advice.

Other difficulties include personal and social elements. Significant others resist the Chicana's growing independence and become threatened. Women often miss dinners and special family occasions because of business commitments.

As a result, they often suffer from guilt and must adjust to juggling diverse responsibilities and commitments. The stresses of building and maintaining a business may also cause women to lose partners.

Latinas leave corporate America because they find themselves "boxed in." They cannot go any higher within the corporate structure. The Hispanic female entrepreneur goes through everything the Anglo female goes through, but she has the added difficulty of being a minority, and at home dealing with different cultural values. The Hispanic female has the burden of constantly moving between two cultures because in the end, says Rodriguez (Olivera, 1989), she has to "make it" in both the Chicano and Anglo cultures.

The final issue—indeed, the overall task—facing the Hispanic female professional is for her to establish a life of her own, balancing social responsibility, individualism, competition, and being a Hispanic female living in both Hispanic and Anglo cultures while struggling against the power and control of men in both cultures. One would think the Chicana would go crazy, but she does not. Some Chicanas have managed to succeed in all spheres. Others have done well in one or two spheres. Yet others are stalemated in arenas they dislike. The success of women is blatantly uneven, and this, of course, flies in the face of simplistic Chicana stereotypes. This also raises the issue of the need for more research, applied research, that addresses or attempts to solve Chicana concerns.

REFERENCES

Davila, Bill. 1988a. "Back to the Future." *Hispanic: The Magazine of the Contemporary Hispanic* (July): 25-27.

______. 1988b. "Hispanic Businesses Growing Fast." *Hispanic: The Magazine of the Contemporary Hispanic* (July): 61.

Olivera, Mercedes. 1989. "The Latina's Juggling Act." *Vista: Focus on Hispanic Americans*, Vol. 4, No. 15 (December 10): 6-13.

Chapter 8

Current Social Issues

Until recently female roles in Hispanic society have been severely limited. In the past the only way the Chicana could maintain respect, the most important cultural variable, was to become a wife and mother or a nun. If a young woman did not conform to one of these roles, she had to endure negative social consequences such as ostracism. The acceptable roles of wife, mother, or nun allowed her personal dignity within a cultural context. These traditional female roles remain very important today. Yet today, while the Chicana maintains her traditional cultural roles, she ventures into nontraditional fields and plays, in addition, nontraditional roles. She is a contemporary woman, involved as a community activist, working in unions and politics to address the issues of poverty, teen pregnancy, and single parenting.

This chapter explores some of the Chicana's fears and failures, as well as some of her successes in discovering new directions. It focuses on contemporary issues affecting the Hispanic woman, her changing roles, and, though minimal, her representation in areas as diverse as the theater, the literary arts, sports, and church affairs.

CHICANAS IN NONTRADITIONAL FIELDS

Although a Chicana is yet to take part in the U.S. space program, the first black female astronaut has emerged. I was somewhat pleasantly surprised to learn that she had a degree in Afro-American studies. The door is somewhat open for minorities, and Chicanas may yet enter this nontraditional field. Sports are an area that is certainly new for Chicanas. Hispanic female professionals are involved in sports nationally and internationally. In this area, for example, one finds Gigi Fernandez, Gabriela Sabatini, and Mary Joe Fernandez as high-ranking tennis players with sizeable incomes *(Hispanic*, 1988). In golf Nancy Lopez is one of the most successful competitors.

Unrelated to sports, yet also areas in which Hispanic women are making inroads, are theater and film. Chicanas and other Latinas are rarely mentioned in theater. Although several Hispanic women have been active, few of them are Chicanas. Playwright and actress Mariairene Forness remains prominent (Zacharia, 1988). She assists in sponsoring playwright contests in order to support Hispanic playwrights and the development of Hispanic theater. Another actress on stage and screen is Carmen Zapata. People know her mostly for her work on television. In spite of good readings she was rejected because she did not look "American" enough (Mejias-Renta, 1989). Early in her acting career she, like many older Hispanic actresses, denied her heritage; but later she reclaimed it with a passion. Zapata's first job at age eighteen was in the chorus of the six-year Broadway run of *Oklahoma*. Some television appearances include "Flamingo Road," "Charlie's Angels," "Marcus Welby, M.D.," and "Villa Alegre Santa Barbara." Carmen Zapata's personal voyage of self-identification has helped create better Latino theater. At the core of her professional career is the Bilingual Foundation of the Arts, a nonprofit community theater group cofounded in 1973 in Los Angeles with Margarita Galban.

Unfortunately, on the stage, on television, and in screen entertainment media few worthwhile roles exist for Hispanic women. When those roles do exist, they fail to portray the truth about Hispanic culture related in those roles. Instead, they promote racial stereotypes, and thus several Chicano actresses have refused to play them. Another problem is the need for Hispanic writers, especially Chicana writers, for the stage and screen and those with capital to invest in the production of relevant work.

There are Chicana writers, of course. Literature is the rapidly growing field for Hispanic women. Most of these women also represent achievement in higher education. Some examples of these women are Sandra Cisneros, Anna Castillo, Maryhelen Ponce, Bernice Zamore, Lorna Dee Cervantes, Angela De Hoyos, Irene I. Blea, Inés Hernandez, and Inés Talemantez. Among Chicanas who do research and literary criticism are Tey Diana Rebolledo, Norma Alarcon, Yvonne Yarbro-Bejarano, Margarita Cota-Cárdenas, Erlinda Gonzales-Berry, Maria

Herrera-Sobek, Cordelia Candelaria, Sonia Saldibar-Hull, Marta Sanchez, and Norma E. Cantu.

FEMINISM AND THE NEXT GENERATION

As activist Chicanas contemplate what to teach Chicanas of the next generation, perhaps the most difficult, yet important task is how to balance two cultures. Contemporary working and professional Chicanas have all the stress experienced by Anglo women plus the stresses and demands of the intersection of race, class, gender, and Chicano culture.

If a complaint is to be hurled at these women, it is that they work very hard and that a few are internalizing Anglo, male-dominated cultural values. Some, not all, are escaping poverty and the working class; but at the same time these few are losing their traditional attitude, the communal approach of helping other Chicanos. In short, in order to make it in Anglo society they had to become or are becoming too individualistic, too profit oriented, too upwardly mobile. Note the word *too*. Some degree of individualism is accepted in Chicano culture, but there is a point at which one stops being Chicano and internalizes Anglo values.

Professional Chicanas have a variety of problems in their personal lives. Their divorce and remarriage rate is high. In small gatherings they complain about being able to talk with family only on a small number of topics. They also complain about men, the lack of Chicana friends and peers. Loneliness and the fear of growing old alone are characteristic problems.

Yet many of these Chicanas feel they have the best of both worlds. They may be criticized for "selling out," but these upwardly mobile women feel they are reaping maximum benefits, the richest form of life, by drawing from two rich cultures. The result is that Chicano women are ideologically divided by the forces at work in their societies.

One test of this conclusion is the position on accepting Coors Corporation funding for special projects that assist the Chicano and Chicana community. Some of the women refer to such funding as "blood money." Others, you will recall, feel it is okay to take the money and not drink the beer; whereas still others feel it is not okay to accept the money under any circumstances. The Coors issue and earlier boycotts have divided the Chicano community for years, and women are certainly a part of that controversy.

THE IMPACT OF THE WOMEN'S MOVEMENT

By drawing guidance from the women's movement, Chicanas have gained some role diversity and upward mobility. One must question, however, whether upward mobility should be the sole measure of broadened roles for Chicanas. There is still not much camaraderie between Chicanas and Anglo women, although several women across the nation are working to change this.

Chicanas feel that Anglo women are frequently preferred over Chicanas and Chicanos for jobs and other rewards. The Chicano community is still relatively disempowered and some Anglo women contribute to this. Many Anglo women have not yet effectively dealt with their racism and class discrimination and they interrupt conversations and walk in front of Chicanas without excusing themselves. Chicanas further recognize that many Anglo women have internalized Anglo male standards, and that many of them want a share of the power, status, and prestige only for themselves or for other Anglo women. Finally, Chicanas have endured degrading treatment and condescending attitudes from ambitious Anglo women, and they know that many Anglo females continue to mistreat Chicano children in classrooms, where they far outnumber Chicanas as teachers, principals, administrators, and professors.

LATINO CHILDREN

Although many Chicanas do not have children, their issues are linked with those of children. In 1989 Latino leaders protested the lack of Hispanics on the thirty-five-member National Commission on Children, appointed by President Bush. The task of the commission was to draft a plan of action on the problems of American youth. Latinos called the failure to incorporate Hispanics inexcusable, citing the great number of Hispanic children in the country and noting that Hispanics are overrepresented among the poor and the high school dropouts.

Latinos found the lack of Hispanics on the National Commission on Children further inexcusable because of the potential impact of the commission. It is to present to the president of the United States and Congress recommendations to correct the problems and deficiencies in the areas of health, education, social services, income, and tax policy. Not to be represented on the commission would mean not to have input into public policy that would affect the welfare of the children of the nation.

Consider some demographics about Latino children. Hispanic children increasingly come from single-female-headed households. The U.S. Bureau of the Census projects there will be 5.5 million more Hispanic children in 2030 than there were in 1985. Education at all levels will be tremendously affected because there are destined to be many more children of color in schools than there will be Anglo children. In fact, concerns regarding Latino children include Latino diversity. For Hispanics of various backgrounds have settled in different regions of the country at different times in U.S. history. The environmental, regional, and historical characteristics of their children vary from group to group; and they do not always have the same sociopolitical concerns.

Key among child-feminist issues are the reproductive rights of women and the quality of life for children. Contemporary childhood is different from that of the childhood of contemporary mothers. Unlike their mothers, who were free to explore their barrios, most children today are no longer free to play or interact in their own homes and yards for fear of abduction, physical or sexual abuse, or even gunfire. Today's children are much less free to roam through their neighborhoods for fear of being gunned down in a drive-by shooting or in some other gang-related activity.

Chicana grandmothers worry over the choices available to their children and their children's children. When they themselves were growing up, there were fewer choices. And when there was a choice, generally the answer was no: no to sex, no to leaving home at a young age, no to boyfriends, no to most choices outside those that would define women as "good girls." Divorce, drugs, and alcohol abuse took place, but they carried such social sanctions that to engage in them was to engage in extraordinary deviant activity. Today these issues are mixed in with quality-of-life and educational concerns for children and their mothers.

With well over 50 percent of Hispanic youth dropping out of school every year, the dropout rate is a matter that goes beyond the interests of Hispanics alone. It affects the entire nation. Youth, including minority youth, build the future of a nation; and our nation has not invested in the largest, youngest segment of youth: Hispanic youth, especially Hispanic females. Well over 50 percent of this youthful population is female.

TEEN PREGNANCY

Children continue on the contemporary scene of feminist concerns. Rated first among them is the high teen pregnancy rate and its link to the school dropout rate. A lack of success in school often leads to teen pregnancy and thus to poverty among women and children. Hispanic women have one of the highest fertility rates in the country. This means they have more babies than most other women in the United States. It has also been documented that the Latino rate of children raising children is high.

The blame for teen pregnancy has been placed on the lack of birth control and birth control information. Others believe it is the lack of parental consent to use birth control. Many more think it is because the Hispanic population tends to be Catholic, and the Catholic religion condemns the practice of birth control. However, one finds that birth control is available, that teenagers are informed about it, and that they know how to use it. Further, many Hispanic Catholics are faithful to their church, yet they do practice birth control.

The reasons given for teenagers having babies often focuses on parents and a dysfunctional family structure. Yet many good parents have instilled in their children the value of abstaining from sex until they reach a proper age, and they have provided good homes for their children to live in; even these Hispanic households have had to deal with teen pregnancy, however.

Hispanics and non-Hispanics alike blame the young people themselves. Many say that teenagers who get pregnant are stupid, irresponsible, or just simply do not care. It has been my experience, though, that today's teens are intelligent, creative, and fun; and that they do care. They care very much. Some of them are indeed careless or irresponsible and believe that pregnancy happens to someone else. But irresponsibility is a characteristic of youth, not gender, class, or race (ethnicity).

Much blaming takes place. When the girls are not blamed, the boys are. Certainly most young men have not accepted sexual responsibility; all too often, boys walk away from pregnant girls only to impregnate another young woman. Meanwhile, girls may suffer ostracism, physical discomfort, and a lifetime of frustration, hard work, and poverty. A pregnant girl's parents endure embarrassment, economic hardship, and family disruption. Many girls go on welfare. Certainly, many young men also suffer; but it is the young women and/or their parents who usually raise the baby.

The stereotype is that pregnant teen girls have loose morals, are "easy." This is not true. Hispanic young women accept motherhood and child-rearing as positive values. Sometimes they are very conservative. Often, though, their attitudes and their behavior are not consistent. But inconsistency is also a characteristic of youth, not gender, class, or race (ethnicity). Only growing up cures this inconsistency. Of course, gender roles for women, especially young Hispanic women, have changed. The social messages and sexual standards that prevented older women from getting pregnant no longer serve as a deterrent in today's society. Today's teen has less restraint and many more choices.

Although these reasons partly explain teen pregnancy, they are not sufficient. There is another approach, an institutional approach, that looks at the social status of young people in today's society. Young people have been displaced from contributing to society. In the "old days" young people worked long, hard hours on farms or in city households and family-owned businesses. Social and technological change has displaced teens from work that diverted sexual energy, and has permitted them to coast. They have thus lost their value in society. Relegated to spending most of their time in school, Hispanic teens face educational frustration and often years of social degradation. Perhaps pregnancy is the resulting symptom, for the reason most frequently cited for dropping out of school is pregnancy. Thus teen pregnancy and the high dropout rate are closely related.

YOUTH AND EDUCATION

Into the minds of some teens come doubts about the contradiction of the American dream and socially degrading messages. They cannot conform to the lies of society shouted in every media message, to the oppressive, confining, artificial structure of school and the American dream that does not appear to be for them. They resist placing synthetic value on lies, things that are unimportant, uninteresting, and totally irrelevant, is recognized as a waste of time. When people are young, they think they know what they want. Hispanic youth are like anyone else in this regard. They realize the importance of graduating, but ending the oppression of the educational system is their most immediate goal. They think they know what they want.

A typical dropout is a "pushout" and, in several ways, sophisticated. Teens who drop out of school because of pregnancy retain dignity and respect. They also gain adult status by producing a child. At the same time, no one knows if they could have passed in school. Dropping out saves them the stress of trying, of failing, and sometimes of feeling guilty for having succeeded when so many fail.

A child who drops out, however, exchanges short-term pain (at least twelve years in school) for long-term suffering (a lifetime). This generally comes in the form of a life of poverty and lack of opportunity. Teens know this. Yet such is the pain of being young and in school that they choose immediate relief and thus to endure the consequences. Their most immediate goal is to receive affirmation as valued human beings. They find this in the arms of another young person with the same need.

What about abortion for the pregnant teen? Abortion has not been an alternative for most Chicanas. In fact, the Chicano community has been divided on abortion. The 1980s saw some agreement with the Reagan position on the question of legalized abortion. Rodolfo O. De la Garza and Robert R. Brischetto (1983) noted that 47 percent of the Hispanics in their sample favored legalized abortion under certain circumstances, whereas 34 percent opposed abortion under any circumstances. (Also see Sierra, 1988.)

1989 marks the sixteenth anniversary of the U.S. Supreme Court's historic *Roe v. Wade* decision legalizing abortion. Some women charge that language was softened to hide the truth about abortions. They compare what happened to the Jews in Germany to what happens to the unborn's civil right to life. At Right to Life demonstrations many signs bear the symbols that have become associated with antiabortion protests. Pictures of the formed but unborn fetus in its early stages are depicted. However, Chicanas have not been highly visible at either right-to-life or pro-choice activities.

The question remains: How do we prevent teen pregnancy? My answer is affirmation, affirmation, affirmation. Teach children that they are valuable. Teach them that they are the most important element of our society, the future. Teach them that there are members of the Hispanic society who have devoted a lifetime to social change. Some have died in order to make opportunities available to young people. Teach young people the communal value of being linked to a whole much greater than the individual. Teach them that they have social responsibility because they are alive; as human beings our role is to leave this world a better place, not take as much as we can without giving back anything. Finally, teach young people to give their very best, especially when it comes to having and raising children. Talk to them about love and the difference between love and sex. When we love others, we want to give them our very best. Love is not enough. Relationships and having babies require economic, social, and spiritual resources developed over time. Into this period of time must be placed energy in thinking, planning, and working on oneself and on one's life. Teenagers are not in a position to offer to participate in life-giving activities when they lack resources to bring to a relationship.

To be healthy people, Chicano youth need to retain the cultural values that distinguish them from Anglos: the combination of personal dignity and respect for others. Traditional Hispanics give respect to all who are born because they are born. They are resistant to taking it away. This ideology is more fluid than Anglo ideology, for in Chicano culture dignity and respect are ascribed at birth. In Anglo culture they are an achieved status; they are earned.

GRASSROOTS MOVEMENTS AS HOLISTIC MOVEMENTS

Around the country grassroots organizations address issues like teen pregnancy, AIDS, police brutality, and the rights of workers, women, and children. Most of these organizations are holistic; that is, they address several concerns in an integrated fashion. Also, many national organizations began as grassroots movements. Among existing national organizations of mixed origin are the American G.I. Forum, AT&T-Hispa, Congressional Hispanic Caucus Institute, Hispanic Chamber of Commerce, Hispanic Bar Association, Hispanic Organization of Postal Employees (HOPE), Latin League of United Latin-American Citizens (LULAC), Mexican-American Legal Defense and Educational Fund (MALDEF), Mexican-American Women's National Association (MANA), National Coalition of Hispanic Health and Human Services (COSSMHO), National Council of La Raza, and National Democratic Hispanic Caucus.

Standing out from the rest is the United Farm Workers (UFW). In 1988 and 1989 the question of physical violence became, once again, very real to Chicanas, particularly to activist Dolores Huerta, vice-president of the UFW. Huerta was violently attacked while involved in a peaceful demonstration outside a San Francisco hotel, where George Bush was attending a campaign dinner. The demonstration in which Huerta was involved protested Bush's statement that he would not support the UFW boycott of California table grapes.

The grape boycott has for many years been a nonviolent action aimed at bringing public attention to unfair labor laws and government use of deadly pesticides. The protest targeting Bush drew attention to the birth defects, cancer, and poisoning of workers. Cancer among children was an immediate concern. There are documented cases of severe birth defects of children born to parents who harvest table grapes. Since 1984 in McFarland, California, the heart of the richest agricultural area, five children have developed some form of cancer and six more have died. These pesticides are also passed on to consumers when they purchase and consume the fruit.

At the Bush demonstration Huerta suffered life-threatening injuries at the hands of police officers. It is ironic that the UFW has always employed nonviolent means to relate its message and has, in the process, incurred violence. Aurora Camacho de Schmidt (1988), an American Friends Service Committee worker in Philadelphia, maintains that the history of the UFW is the history of a nonviolent movement that goes beyond immediate gains in the labor field. This movement addresses various social, economic, and political concerns. Violence, however, has been at the heart of this movement because it dares to question the growers and attempts to bargain over the right to work, wages, and safety conditions. These interests have been addressed since the 1920s and 1930s, by Chicanas and Chicanos in the labor movement.

Chicanas have been involved in farm worker issues since the beginning. In the past Dolores Huerta's contributions have been overshadowed by media coverage of Cesas Chavez, his demonstrations, and his fasts, for the media focus on men in leadership positions. However, equally involved and committed in the struggle to organize a union and promote negotiations with corporate farmers is Dolores Huerta. She has worked side by side with Chavez, and many other women, in boycotts, strikes, demonstrations, pickets, and sit-ins. Huerta has contributed to lobbying for changes in child welfare, health, and education. Furthermore, she and her colleagues have extended those efforts to include all migrants, regardless of race, ethnicity, or color. They have also withstood criticism and physical abuse at the hands of elitist racists and sexists.

An issue closely related to farm workers, but one that also sadly affects highly urbanized communities, is poverty. Poverty among Latinos (especially their children) has increased at a rate faster than for the rest of the nation (Sierra, 1988). In 1980 35 percent of all Latino children under the age of six lived in poverty. By 1983, 42 percent of Latino children under the age of six were poor. The number grows each day.

Poverty is also a feminist issue, tied to women's overall economic concerns about unemployment and inflation and revealed in Chicana attitudes regarding social issues. Thus, feminist Chicanas generally favor increased spending on social programs including bilingual education, the extension of the Voting Rights Act, reproductive freedom, and, to a lesser degree, the passage of the Equal Rights Amendment.

HOLISTIC HEALTH AND HEALING

The tendency to work holistically is a Chicana characteristic. Women have always been a viable part of Mexican-American health and healing. Chicana medicine has integrated physical, emotional, and spiritual or religious components. Herbs, massage, ritual, and prayer are part of the approach. Many foods are used for medicinal purposes but techniques vary with specialization. *Rezadoras* pray and can be called faith healers. *Sobaderas* are massage therapists and sometimes chiropractors. *Parteras* are midwives and sometimes gynecologists. *Curanderas* are general practitioners who heal at the emotional, spiritual, and physical levels.

Perhaps the best-known health delivery person is the *curandera*. She has for some time caught the attention of Anglo anthropologists, sociologists, and health care professionals. In Southwest mental health centers *curanderas* are sometimes incorporated as part of the therapeutic staff and utilized in the treatment of psychiatric patients. One *curandera*, Diana Velazquez of Denver, Colorado, has gained so much recognition that she now gives guest lectures and holds workshops in foreign countries on Chicano health and healing practices. There has been much written on the subject of *curanderismo*, but the best source for information on the power and practice of *curanderas* is Robert Trotter II and Juan A. Chavera's *Curanderismo: Mexican-American Folk Healing* (1981).

Many medical studies, like the one cited above, have been done in Texas, usually where there is much poverty, a large Mexican-American population, and few medical facilities. From the literature one would assume that only uneducated, unsophisticated people with few resources who live near the U.S.-Mexican border use *curanderismo*. This is not true. The use of *curanderismo* is widespread, and not only among Mexican Americans, because it works. In these medical studies the tendency is to focus on the population and its medical practices and not on the dominant sociocultural system of discrimination that does not provide health services to these areas.

Aida Hurtado gives insight into the practice of *parteras* in Hidalgo County, Texas (1987). Hurtado concludes that not only are Chicanas helping women to deliver their babies, they are also providing rudimentary health care for the expectant mother and her infant. South Texas has a significant shortage of both professional and associate health personnel, and the Anglo-dominated system has not been inviting to the Chicano. In addition, Anglo health and healing approaches are not multifaceted or holistic, and some Chicanos use the system as a last resort.

Although many studies cite cultural and language differences as the primary reason for underutilization of the system by Chicanos, Hurtado's findings were different. There were no cultural reasons given. The decision to use a *partera* was mostly influenced by economic and situational factors. This is an important point because the Americanization period produced and cemented a class structure in the Southwest that blocked Chicano participation in the ongoing systems.

Those with resources tend to receive better health care. Social scientists and other health researchers have been too quick to blame Chicano culture not only for lack of medical care but also for low levels of attainment in education, employment, and politics. This blaming-the-victim perspective continues even though Chicano and other scholars have warned against it for over twenty years.

The literature on the use of health facilities among Chicanos is incomplete and frequently fails to indicate the degree to which Chicanos use Anglo health professionals. In fact, there is a lack of evidence on how often Chicanos use the dominant health system. Personal experience indicates it is widely used primarily because Chicanos and Chicanas are not learning traditional health and healing methods and because "unnatural" (manmade) illness has evolved from urban stress and toxins. Anglos have introduced cancer-producing agents and other rare health hazards into the environment.

Solutions for Chicano underutilization of dominant healthcare systems generally concentrate on changing the beliefs and behaviors of Mexican Americans. There has been no movement to have Anglos change their beliefs and behaviors or to blend Chicano approaches to health and healing with the Anglo health system. The arrogant assumption by those representing the Anglo system is that the system does not have to change; it is the individual, or Chicano, response to that system that must change. Basic to their stance is that Chicanos have nothing to teach, nothing to contribute to the arena of science.

The midwives in Hurtado's article, however, were more willing to cooperate, economically and otherwise, with women in various circumstances. Very few health professionals would deliver babies for such a low fee. In 1987 the average savings was $467.90 per delivery. The *partera*'s annual income was between $200 and $400. Most *parteras* deliver at the patient's home, a more supportive, natural environment. Mentored by older women, they honor the cultural practice of burying the placenta and umbilical cord. Some Mexicanas and Chicanos tend to believe that the afterbirth is human flesh and that burial is the only way to dispose of it. Also, if it is not buried, the female may become infertile.

Some women in Hurtado's study traveled from Mexico to the United States to give birth to their babies. This political act gave the child U.S. citizenship: the rights and privileges and opportunity to live and work in the United States. This also gave the women more of an advantage in obtaining visas, moving to Texas, having more children, and obtaining U.S. citizenship herself. These women sought U.S. citizenship to escape intense poverty and hardship in Mexico; they failed to note that with citizenship came discrimination against Mexican-Americans.

Key contemporary health concerns for Hispanic women have been brought forth by the Hispanic Women's Health Association. Some concerns have been developing a Hispanic woman's health agenda, creating relevant health policies for Hispanic women and their families, curbing the increase of tuberculosis, helping the Hispanic female accept health care, and expanding health insurance coverage to uninsured Hispanic families. In addition, the association has focused attention on the second-generation, female single parent, cardiovascular risk reduction, diabetes, substance abuse, and the implementation of community-based IVDU (intravenous drug use) AIDS risk reduction programs. Foremost is the IVDU AIDS concern. At least 21 percent of Hispanic women have AIDS. Also high is the AIDS level among Hispanic children born to mothers with AIDS. Of all AIDS cases, Hispanic children account for 24 percent (Maldonado, 1989). These cases are largely due to the use of shared needles among self-administering intravenous drug users who are the sexual partners of Hispanic women. Although Hispanic women engage in intravenous drug use, it is primarily a male activity. Generally, women with AIDS contract their disease from sexual partners who are drug addicted.

RELIGIOUS AND SPIRITUAL CONCERNS

Although Chicanas have struggled to become a more viable part of the religious rites of the Catholic church, they have not emerged to question and confront the male domination of that institution and the power of the pope. If ever an area warranted a more radical feminist perspective, the Catholic church certainly warrants it. This, of course, is not to discredit the brave women who have functioned within the context of the church to bring about change in this institution. They, indeed, have struggled and have brought about some change; but lay Chicanas have not made this a burning feminist issue.

Yet Chicana feminists point to the Catholic church as one of the most oppressive institutions in their culture. It is charged with exerting influence in not allowing women to define their own secular and spiritual lives. Feminists also say the church resists change and is oppressive in not recognizing the dissolution of marriages, in taking a firm stance against birth control and abortion, and in not allowing women to be priests.

But the most urgent contemporary concern in the Catholic church is the need to recruit more priests. Some cultural reasons explain why Chicanos are not attracted to the priesthood. The high value placed on family and children contradicts the church's requirement of celibacy and is often cited as the reason Mexican-American males are no longer attracted to the priesthood.

Another area of activity is that most frequently referred to as liberation theology. Many young men simply do not see an opportunity to assist their community via the priesthood. Liberation theology is also affecting the behavior of women in the church. The Chicano civil rights movement of the 1960s had much to do with this change. During this time many priests and community members approached the church to assist in addressing the issues of racism and sexism in the church. The church was at best resistant. At its worst it denied Chicanos support. This experience was widespread. It angered and alienated many members of the Hispanic community. Consequently, many, many Chicanos, including priests, left the Catholic church. Some left for more fundamentalist faiths. Others developed their own spirituality or abandoned religion altogether.

Because Mexican-American culture is ritualistic and highly symbolic, Hispanics in the Catholic church have explored and implemented use of the Spanish language, music, art, and traditional symbols in an effort to retain parishioners. For example, tortillas have even been used as the host during communion.

Chicanas are exploring ways in which their spiritual roots and cultural identities shape their faith. Other feminist dialogues include the ordination of women as priests, and whether the church is an instrument of oppression or liberation. The concern over goddesses as representative of Chicana theological perspectives or the need of their recognition has not been as active an issue as it has been in Anglo feminist circles. Those active in the Catholic church are quick to point out that Nuestra Señora de Guadalupe (Our Lady of Guadalupe) is a significant female deity with both Indian and Spanish-European characteristics. They would like this holy image to be more fully incorporated into religious services outside the Chicano community.

Even when recent overtures have been made to the Chicano community on behalf of the church, the critical community asserts the church has made only weak attempts. Chicanas note a class element to Hispanic concerns in the Catholic church, which tends to be characterized by a middle-class population. Most, but not all, Catholic Hispanics are working-class or very poor. This inconsistency places Chicanos at a disadvantage in the church.

A CHANGING FOCUS

Perhaps there is a move toward less holistic organizations. Perhaps this happens when Chicanas interact with the dominant systems and are not in opposition to it. One area in which some single-vision or single-issue organizing takes place is in specific political endeavors. Traditionally, the area of politics by its very nature was holistic for Chicanos. This is why it was so important to the country and to Chicanas specifically.

Public opinion studies show that Chicanos favored a decrease in spending for defense, space programs, and foreign aid. In 1988 they opposed U.S. military aid to the government of El Salvador and to the Contras in Nicaragua (Sierra, 1988). All of these positions ran counter to the Reagan administration. Ironically, during the Reagan administration Republicans made some inroads into the traditional Democratic Chicano vote. Gender differences among Hispanic voters did not distinguish voting patterns in the presidential election. Hispanic women and men disliked Reagan equally. In contrast, gender-difference patterns appeared very strongly in the general U.S. population, but especially among Puerto Ricans. In these cases, women showed more disapproval of, or less support for, Reagan than did their male counterparts.

Former state senator from Colorado Polly Baca has been mentioned, but a Hispanic woman whose name has also been connected with politics, and who is highly controversial, is Linda Chavez. One of Chavez's first political jobs was with Democrat Polly Baca. More recently Chavez has changed political affiliation and was the president of the U.S. English movement. She became symbolic of Hispanics leading an organization promoting English as the official language of the United States. Her efforts delighted those who supported the cause but infuriated those who opposed it. Chavez ultimately resigned her position. She did so, not because she had a change of mind about the importance of maintaining a common language in the United States, but because the founder of the U.S. English movement undermined her ability to defend the organization against charges that it was anti-Hispanic (*Hispanic Link Weekly Report*, 1988).

There is little agreement on where Latinas should place their feminist efforts. Why should there be agreement? This is a highly diverse group of women. The recent matter of abortion and the Equal Rights Amendment has motivated the second generation of Chicana feminists to attempt to work with the National Organization of Women (NOW). But leaders of Latina organizations report that NOW is not representing their agenda. At the heart of the matter is the priority of issues and the racism that Latinas are still experiencing within that organization. NOW has not effectively dealt with women of color and their issues. In 1989 NOW's thirty-two-member board of directors included three Latinas: Olga Vives of Illinois, Annabelle Jaramillo of Oregon, and Ginny Montes of Georgia. Six of the board members are black (*Hispanic Link Weekly Report*, 1989). Where NOW seeks to elevate Anglo women to equal Anglo men in all aspects of life, Hispana feminists aim at equalizing male-female power within a Hispanic-community context, elevating the quality of life within that context to that of Anglos in U.S. society.

The consensus among Latina leaders is that NOW focuses on issues that do not address the Latina's concern with basic survival: education, job training, housing, and childcare. Anglo women describe Hispanic women as typically more conservative about gay rights, abortion, and other issues espoused by NOW. This "conservatism" has not yet been addressed and certainly is not representative of all Chicanas. Loretta Ross, director of NOW's women-of-color program in 1989, maintains that many Hispanic women have difficulty dealing with issues of sexuality. At this time, this premise has no basis. It needs to be questioned and researched. It could be that Anglo women are viewing Chicanas through Anglo eyes, not feminist eyes.

Esther Favole, president-elect of the Coalition of Hispanic American Women in Miami (*Hispanic Link Weekly Report*, 1989), stresses the feminist need for Latinas to be seen by males in professional positions. She feels this would sensitize them to accepting women in leadership roles. Lourdes Saab, executive director of the Hispanic Women's Council in Los Angeles, feels that women's organizations get support from traditional male groups, but more headway needs to be made. She also stresses the battle between the intellectual and the cultural advancement of men: "The intellectual is winning, but the cultural battle is still being waged on the home front, behind closed doors."

Indeed, Chicana feminists still struggle with the Hispanic male perception of female roles. While some men during the 1960s and 1970s accepted feminism, their contemporaries were not always as accepting. But economic, social, and political needs are slowly eroding the macho mentality. Nevertheless, many young men in many barrios still desire women who will not challenge their perceived male superiority. These Hispanic men must deal with the fact that women's roles have changed and will continue to change.

REFERENCES

Camacho de Schmidt, Aurora. 1988. "Violence and a Non-Violent Movement." *Hispanic Link Weekly Report*, Vol. 6, No. 44 (November 7):4.

Chavez, Linda. 1988. "U.S. English Should Chart New Course." *Hispanic Link Weekly Report*, Vol. 6, No. 44 (November 7): 3.

De la Garza, R., and R. Brischetto. 1983. "The Mexican-American Electorate: Information Sources and Policy Orientations." Occasional Paper No. 2, San Antonio, Texas, Southwest Voter Registration Education Project and the Hispanic Population Studies Program of the Center for Mexican-American Studies. Austin: University of Texas. 9-10.

Garcia, John. 1984. "Chicano Political Development." In *1984 National Roster of Hispanic Elected Officials*. Arizona State University. 11.

Hispanic: The Magazine of the Contemporary Hispanic. 1988. "Women: The Contradiction" (July): 29-33, 66-69.

Hispanic Link Weekly Report, 1989. "NOW Misses Mark with Most Hispanic Feminists," Vol. 7, No. 15 (April 10): 1-3.

Hurtado, Aida. 1987. "Midwife Practices in Hidalgo County, Texas." *Trabajos Monográficos: Studies in Chicana/Latina Research*, Vol. 3, No. 1: 1-30.

Maldonado, Irma C. 1989. "President's Message." *MANA Newsletter*, Vol. 6, No. 2 (Spring): 1 & 4.

Mejias-Renta, Antonio. 1989. "The Coming Home of Carmen Zapata." *Vista*, Vol. 6, No. 3 (March 12): 5-6.

Olivera, Mercedes. 1989. "The Latina's Juggling Act." *Vista: Focus on Hispanic Americans*, Vol. 4, No. 15 (December 10): 6-13.

Sierra, Christine Marie. 1988. "Chicano Politics after 1984." In Juan R. Garcia, Julia Curry Rodriguez, and Clara Lomas, eds., *Times of Challenge: Chicanos and Chicanas in American Society*. Houston: University of Houston Press, Mexican-American Studies Program, Monograph Series No. 6. 7-24.

Trotter, Robert, II, and Juan A. Chavera. 1981. *Curanderismo, Mexican-American Folk Healing*. Athens, Ga.: University of Georgia Press.

Vista: Focus on Hispanic America (March 12, 1989): 14.

Zacharia, Cory. 1988. "Still in the Center: Mariairene Fornes." *Hispanic: The Magazine of the Contemporary Hispanic* (July): 44-46.

Chapter 9

Theoretical Perspectives on the Intersection of Gender, Class, and Ethnicity

This chapter asserts positive value in studying racism, sexism, and class discrimination in the life of La Chicana. It attempts to update general theories of discrimination by drawing from the academic work of La Chicana, racial and ethnic minorities, and feminist scholars to propose that there are many levels of social interaction affected by U.S. value systems. Certainly the analysis of La Chicana provides the social sciences with a holistic, multidimensional perspective. To use this perspective, however, the social sciences must rid themselves of biases against feminist and minority scholarship. They must accept that racial and ethnic minorities and women have something of value to teach.

To discuss the intersection of social variables that describe the life of La Chicana, it is first necessary to examine the racism, sexism, and class status in U.S. society. It is also necessary to examine current scholarship, focusing on the institutionalized inequalities and political use of research in academia. These internalized inequalities have cost U.S. social scientists their position of international leadership, which will be further discussed in the next chapter.

This chapter goes beyond the review of racism, sexism, and class discrimination to contend that a large segment of the Chicana population has been active in creating social change not only in the Chicano community but in the social sciences as well. The Chicana has not been recognized because of her interdisciplinary theoretical approach toward the social sciences and her ideas of liberation from an oppressed condition. She also takes a holistic approach, including spiritual elements, to analyze race (ethnicity), class, and gender.

A REVIEW OF CLASS STRUCTURE

The treatment of the poor serves as a warning to U.S. workers. Poor people are always available as cheap labor for the ruling elite, particularly in a crisis when the social system needs more workers. But when it needs less workers, the poor move into a reserve labor pool to await further employment Poverty, however, makes jobs for many middle-class people. For example, middle-class people have jobs helping poor people; they are social workers, welfare workers, educational and job counselors, food stamp distributors, and medicaid and medicare officers. Even teachers, doctors, attorneys, nurses, politicians, and business people have jobs that put them in touch with those in poverty. Many employers, notably the state, make money addressing the needs of the poor.

In the 1960s poverty and racism became hotly debated issues in the United States. Michael Harrington (1963) opened for sociologists the discussion of poverty in the United States. Through Lyndon B. Johnson's War on Poverty and the efforts of the civil rights movement, the country recognized the existence of Chicanos in the nation. That this group was historically downtrodden was a surprise to most people—except to Chicanos, whose poverty had been a well-kept secret from the rest of society.

How do the Chicano working poor live? They have little education and manual jobs with little prestige.Poor Chicanas are the janitors and housekeepers of society. Most are unskilled laborers. Chicana jobs are physically demanding, deadend, and frequently dangerous. Chicanas tend to be migrant workers, dishwashers, and domestics. Women are highly concentrated in service areas as waitresses, laundry and garment workers, department store clerks, and maids in hotels. Frequently they are also heads of households, or may be supplementing another income. Al- though they perform socially necessary labors, these women are severely underpaid and have therefore been classified as the working poor.

And where do these poor live? Chicanas are found in crowded, rundown, cheap housing. Few Chicanas have actually become poor. Most have been born into poverty. Like other poor people, the Chicana poor are relatively invisible, segregated in ghettos, barrios, and other deteriorating communities. They are ignored by political officials and kept out of sight by freeways, factories, railroad yards, and industrial plants—and laws and social pressure.

It is ironic that at the same time poor Chicanas are invisible they also have no privacy because they must secure social services from the government, which makes them reveal intimate elements of their personal lives. This information generally becomes available as data to be used in budgeting and funding, in national annual and biannual reports, and in social science research. Further, the police are ever present in poor communities, where behavior is constantly monitored.

Most Americans blame the poor for their poverty, failing to recognize the discriminatory tendency to use the poor as examples of what happens to those who do not conform to the norm in society. Most drastically punished are those who choose not to conform and those, like people of color, who cannot conform. The consequence is poverty.

The working class lives slightly differently, but it also endures overcrowded, rundown housing. It is further characterized by physical exhaustion. For the working class, as for the poor, the American Dream and all that sustains it promise a better quality of life but do not deliver it. The media uphold these working-class dreams. For most poor and working-class Chicanas, the major life objectives are marriage and work. Marriage promises independence and the hope for a better life. Although educational aspirations are on the increase, Chicano social structure and family pressures may push a young Chicana into early work responsibilities.

These pressures, along with any dysfunctional coping skills, may further diminish the opportunities of working-class Chicanas. While middle-income Chicanas are engaging in sports, hobbies, homework, and dating, poor and working-class Chicanas are frequently working both in and outside the home. Young men and women are frequently in deadend jobs, and young women may be homemakers and mothers as early as the age of sixteen. Thus, while still young, they are subjected to the stresses of paying bills and raising children and have little opportunity to relate to women who are in different roles such as those of writer, actress, professor, scientist, physician, or attorney.

During the recent economic recession many middle-class persons slid into the lower classes. The middle class encompasses white-collar workers and professionals frequently used by the media as role models. Those Chicanos who have successfully climbed into this class act as role models for Chicanos in the lower classes. They also act as a buffer between the lower and upper classes. For an earlier and fuller discussion on the elements of class structure, the reader is referred to the works of Karl Marx, as presented in the work of Frederic Engels (1967), and Max Weber (Gerth and Wright Mills, 1946).

The upper class is very private compared to the middle class, which engages in conspicuous consumption. It has been estimated that this affluent class consists of 1 to 3 percent of the population, but that it controls or owns a minimum of 25 percent of the nation's wealth. These figures may be conservative. For the most part, however, these people inherit wealth, whereas the poor and the middle class usually do not. The wealthy are a tightly knit group consisting of the old rich and the new rich, the old rich having had wealth for generations and the new rich having acquired it only recently. Although they sometimes cross paths, there generally are few relationships between the two groups. The names of wealthy people appear in the *Social Register*. These people have much leisure time and may engage in social philanthropy. Chicano membership in this class is scarce but growing.

DISCRIMINATION BASED ON RACE, CLASS, AND GENDER

There was a time when people thought that what we today call racism was acceptable. However, sociocultural progress by the 1960s encouraged some to feel that to stop racism was the right and moral thing to do. Today, the argument has changed. Racism needs to be stopped, not because of moral rightness, but because it is the economic and politically expedient thing to do. Racial and ethnic minorities will soon be the majority population, and racism costs money. Hispanics are estimated to have at least $98 billion to spend on a variety of commodities, and discrimination is robbing this from the gross national product.

However, there is another reason for doing away with racism: to better our international political power. Because of technology the world has gotten smaller. Technology allows Americans to communicate, if they have a common language, with most people around the world. They can travel and be on the other side of the world in a very few hours.

But the truth is that Americans lack the ability to communicate at the international level. It is the world that has been forced to communicate with the United States. For most Americans are monolingual and, for the most part, monocultural, functioning well in only one culture. This is so at a time when global communication requires bilingual ability and cultural literacy on many fronts. Americans' lack of multilingual skills and multicultural understanding has cost the United States power, status, and prestige in international affairs.

It is in this arena that Chicanos have the advantage and can teach the United States, if it wants to learn. Thus far, the United States has been unwilling to learn about balancing more than one language and more than one culture, and it has in this context mistreated Chicanos. Chicanos frequently report that their bilingual and bicultural abilities have proven worthy in courtrooms, in business transactions, and in settling disputes. Being able to function in at least two languages and two cultures, however, has not to date been a valued characteristic in this country, and Chicanos have not been rewarded for their abilities.

At the international level, America's general failure to value more than its own language and culture has caused strained international relations not only with leaders of Spanish countries but also with other non-English-speaking world leaders. The media notes that meetings of world importance are held in English. Most Americans take pride in this knowledge, viewing the use of English as the language of diplomacy as a victory. They choose to interpret this to mean that the United States is in a powerful position. This is not necessarily true. The sorry truth is that English is used because most American diplomats are not fluent in another language. Most diplomats from other countries, in contrast, can speak more than one language; they engage in English negotiations out of courtesy and lack of choice.

Racism is no longer as profitable for the racist as it once was. In fact, it is costing large corporations, which have become aware they are not receiving maximum production because racism on the job absorbs time, energy, and profit. Most corporations conduct workshops on how racism on the job affects the bottom line: dollars and cents. It seems that to engage in racist behavior is to engage in antiquated behavior. Yet people do. This is perhaps because there is still some payoff. Competition for what are considered to be scarce resources is reduced if minorities and women are eliminated. This allows and sustains the Anglo male advantage. The truth is that resources in society are not scarce. They are simply concentrated in the hands, and bank accounts, of a few, the few who profit from controlling or fragmenting social forces that could make more resources available to more people.

Sexism functions much like racism. The lack of value for women in the society causes oppression of women in several segments of society, as well as a general lack of value for their bodies as much as for social contributions. Abuse is a symptom of sexist discrimination that gives males priority. Like racism, it has become part socialization, so much so that many people feel a division of the genders is good and natural.

Class discrimination, on the other hand, victimizes the poor. Those with resources take advantage and may abuse the poor. Because most things in U.S. society cost money, many people think the poor are powerless in resisting the impositions of the rich. This, however, is not true. Labor unions and poor people's campaigns have been very effective. What some do not realize is that the rich need the poor in order to remain rich. If the poor do not adhere to prescribed roles, the rich do not maximize profit.

With the study of Chicanos has come the realization that Anglos cannot exist in positions of privilege unless people of color exist without privilege. The multisegmented system exerts a push-pull strain to make this system work well. The objective and the consequences of the cumulative effort is different for each segment. There is a dual standard. The minority effort works much harder than the dominant Anglo to live out its limited life chances. This happens while the Anglo effort works to keep itself comfortable.

THE INTERSECTION OF VARIABLES AND THE IMPACT OF CULTURE

The intersection of variables becomes most apparent in the study of discrimination. To be discriminated against because one is a minority group member, generally, produces poverty for the individual or group discriminated against. (The multifaceted cycle of discrimination has been reviewed in Chapter 5.) Discrimination results in low levels of education, poor political participation, and problems with health care and employment. It produces high levels of involvement in the criminal justice system, trapping people in cycles.

Some would say the above cycle produces a culture of poverty. It does not. Poverty is imposed from outside the entity. The factors that most strongly define culture and to which culture gives definition are values, norms, symbols, and communication forms that develop within a group. The group develops symptoms, reactions, and culturally relative coping mechanism to poverty, but it does not originally produce poverty.

Cultural productions are made in art, poetry, music, religion, and other social institutions such as schools and the family. These productions, however, do not exist without being affected by the dominant society's cultural values, some of which demean and degrade the minority group. Frequently what is rendered in cultural productions is how the minority culture deals with hopes, fears, and life and death. Cultural productions may be material but they embody values and ethics. In Chicano culture these productions convey a high regard for family structure and family relationships, for cleanliness, marriage, children, education, the elderly, religion and spirituality, interaction between the sexes, days of significance, and the need for social change.

Yes, the need for social change is a high priority for Chicanos. Perhaps the biggest Chicano fear is that children will be absorbed by dominant American values and that talented Chicanos with resources will be changed, lost to the community and to their families. The biggest hope is, perhaps, that the community will become economically stable, that racism will end, and that Chicano people will be allowed to participate fully in society at large without having to give up their culture or be influenced by racism, sexism, and class discrimination. It is difficult to envision what direction this culture would take given that for 150 years it has had to live with discrimination.

Their culture is important to Chicanos because it sustains them. It gives them shared knowledge and direction. Without cultural references, people are empty; they may feel lost and confused. Without cultural references, individuals may become disoriented and depressed, even suicidal. The person without culture is not rooted and has a difficult time relating beyond the surface. Populations in secondary social positions, especially, need cultural identity for insulation against oppressive forces.

For the Chicana, her culture is also extraordinarily important because it includes rites of passage, those times in a person's life that symbolize movement from one status to another. For Chicanas these include birth, baptism, beginning school, first holy communion, confirmation, *quinceañera*, and marriage and death rituals. In a discussion about women the *quinceañera* is most important. The "coming-out" ritual marks the end of girlhood and grants womanhood status at the age of fifteen.

CHICANAS AND THE AMERICAN DREAM

How racism permeates the society and sets up barriers to upward mobility for people of color has been discussed. Also discussed has been how sexism and class discrimination exist in the same fashion, functioning to fixate a stratified social system. For women, the American Dream of upward mobility is a little different than it is for men. Society socializes its young girls to grow up with intentions to marry and live happily ever after. It also socializes them to make men important social and economic assets in women's lives. Women are not meant to enter the labor market directly, supporting themselves and making other contributions. They are to stimulate the labor market, indirectly, as consumers. The multidimensional manner in which these messages are communicated works. Women are superconsumers. This is why so much advertising is directed toward women. Chicanas are not immune from the messages.

Society brainwashes Chicanas—as it does other women—into thinking they are incomplete and can obtain social worth only if they exist as a media-defined woman: blond, blue-eyed, with a beautiful tall and lean body, a middle-class marriage, and 2.5 children. For a very few Chicanas this ideal has changed, but not for many. For the most part, Chicana socialization, that process of learning culture and the internalization of what has been learned, sustains the artificial importance and dominance of men and the ideal Anglo model of what is considered an attractive or beautiful woman.

Socialization produces a female norm. At the same time it also produces producers of children, the future workers for the capitalist system, and it keeps women in the role of consumer and out of the competitive job market (Benson, 1969, 1981). Prescribed social roles, however, rarely bring all the status, power, and prestige that women believe they will. Fantasies and dreams, especially in marriage, typically remain unrealized (not only for women, of course, but also for men). Nevertheless, women remain addicted to the American Dream, its teachings, its assumptions, and its promises of a good life. Unfortunately, the Dream can come true only if one is born into the norm.

Chicanas are not born into the Anglo norm, however. If they adhere to the social norms, if they behave as Anglos, they may succeed; but they will nonetheless be discriminated against because they are women, and women of color. Even when they appear to be accepted by Anglos, they are accepted only as long as they do not act Chicano. Thus, a Chicana must deny her own identity and take up the identity of the norm. For a fuller discussion on these reactions to discrimination, see the work of Peter Rose (1981).

When a woman accepts the norm, she accepts a gender role: behaviors, rights, and responsibilities assigned to each gender in a culture. When a Chicana accepts the norm in her culture, she accepts that norm as inconsistent with the dominant, Anglo norm. Norms outline a prescribed role for her not only as a woman but also as a Chicana. The norm, then, is her version of the American Dream. Some Chicanas adhere to the dominant American Dream version. Others have a Chicana version.

CONTRIBUTIONS TOWARD THE GROWTH OF THE SOCIAL SCIENCES

How far has the study of La Chicana advanced the social sciences? Social scientists have established that women and men are different, yet very much the same. More often than not, male-female social differences are rooted in perceptions and in degrees of power rather than in reality. Fundamentally, social scientists are interested in understanding the differences in the lives of women and men. The study of relationships, power structures, statuses, and their impact on other social variables has been advanced by the entrance of women into this formerly male-dominated arena.

Mexican-American and black women in the social sciences have made a major contribution concerning women and the lives of people of color. They have provided a multifaceted, or multidimensional, approach to the interaction of social variables. Prior to this approach, the social science perspective was narrow, limiting the holistic understanding of the realities of life.

It was minority women who made it clear to white women, social scientists, and society in general that they were doubly discriminated against, and that the discrimination manifested itself in social activity that inverted and victimized them again. They were victimized first for being people of color, and then for being female. They were further victimized for being poor or lower-class. These factors resulted in limited choices, which in turn meant minority women were left with low levels of education, little political power, low health standards, low employment, and high involvement with the criminal justice system.

A FUNCTIONAL DIVISION OF GENDER ROLES

Perhaps Mexican-Americans are still adhering more to traditional sex roles. One cannot analyze Chicano gender roles using Anglo values. One cannot point an accusing finger by charging Mexican-American men with sexism and Mexican-American women with passivity. It is true that like other U.S. cultures this population has strong social prescriptions, but earlier discussions demonstrate that other factors intervene. Mexican-American women lost status, power, and prestige after the Mexican-American War. Their communities were disempowered (Garcia, 1981), they had fewer resources, and their sense of what could be done with their personal lives was diminished.

A division of gender roles in Chicano culture is sometimes needed in order to sustain an upwardly mobile standard of living under severe social conditions. A review of the literature on La Chicana and the Chicano family will reveal a stereotyped picture of a woman in the role of wife and mother, a woman who is docile, passive, uncomplaining, all-suffering, all-forgiving and hard-working (Melville, 1980). She is often presented as the victim of a violent, unfaithful male (Kiev, 1968). Perhaps this is how people would like to perceive La Chicana, and perhaps some of the stereotypes possess elements of truth. However, Chicanas are not what they are presented to be. They are not more abused than are white women, nor are they endowed with the animalistic qualities projected in the stereotypes.

In communal Chicano culture people depend on one another in order to maintain a healthy standard of living. Thus, women must depend more on men and men must depend more on women. It is still a fact, for example, that Anglos have higher earning than Chicanos; women in the United States tend to earn roughly sixty-three cents compared to every male dollar. Chicanas earn less than Anglo females. Extremely low Chicano earnings call for most couples to work to barely meet the essential needs of their families. This is not sexism. This is survival. Both sexes depend on each other to provide status and protection from the harsh, sometimes violent, realities of minority status. The Anglo population does not have to contend to the same degree with this multi-faceted concern.

Women in Chicano culture are strong, strong as cultural and decision-making symbols and strong physically. Cultural and historical social conditions have demanded that both sexes develop strong characters and work hard. For a fuller discussion of the working-class man, see the work of Studs Terkel (1974). Both men and women value homelife. Women are not hesitant to work alongside men in maintaining their home. After working long hours during the week (longer than most white men for the same pay), Chicano men do not hesitate to do physical work around their homes; and, increasingly, men are becoming involved in childrearing.

Chicanos are predominantly working class. Although their earnings are low, they have internalized a work ethic somewhat like the dominant work ethic: They believe that hard work brings upward mobility. Their common racial and ethnic experience has oppressed these hard-working people into their class status. This experience often defuses the gender role issue so important in Anglo society. The shared oppression does not motivate women and men to create distance from one another. Thus, Chicano females and males struggle within their culture over gender issues but struggle together against oppressive forces from the outside.

The reader should not be misguided in thinking that sexism does not exist in Chicano society. Men have adopted and have sustained preferential positions and treatment in Chicano culture because their life is more comfortable this way. This tendency does not begin with Anglo political imposition. As has been related in previous chapters, it immigrated with the Spanish European. The more urbanized and the more assimilated Chicanos become, the more the power differential between Chicano women and men increases. For U.S.-born Chicanos, the form this has taken recently is more American than Mexican.

Even at birth Chicano females and males do not start out the same. Boy babies are still preferred. After birth the genders experience different roles, but it is life chances that become important. Because females bear children, men do not have to endure being subjected to discriminatory health standards, practices, and systems in delivery rooms across the nation; it is women who bear the unusually heavy burden. Unlike white women, Chicanas have more children and are therefore subjected to delivery rooms more frequently than are Anglo women.

Chicano men, like white men, feel women are responsible for birth control; and like white men, they feel women should have primary responsibility for raising children. Unlike that in the dominant society, this opinion is based more on the cultural importance of women than it is rooted in releasing men from childrearing responsibility. On the surface this appears as blatant sexism, but frequently it is not. In part, the indigenous elements of Chicano culture support matriarchy and the strong cultural roles of women.

As noted earlier, a social attempt has been made to treat the Chicano male as black males have been treated. Discrimination works to emasculate black men, and Chicano males have been treated as black men, to make them feel inferior by denying them the symbols of masculinity. This tactic of disempowering and withholding income and other resources has worked to some degree. Chicano males frequently abandon women and children, leaving women to rear children with no support. Because women have internalized beliefs about what men are supposed to provide for them, they turn on Chicano men and place additional social pressure on them.

Perhaps the most important factor in a discussion on sexism is life expectations. Sexist social tendencies manifest themselves in terms of sexist life expectancies and life chances. Anglo men have a shorter life expectancy than white women even though as men they have preferential treatment and increased life chances. They live to an average age of 70.8 years, whereas Anglo women live to roughly 78.2 years. The cut in lifespan for Anglo males is probably attributed to the stress inherent in male culture: the strive for upward mobility, competition, individualism, and even sustaining the status quo. Practicing denial, sexism, and racism also takes its toll. Yet the years Anglo males do live are more comfortable for them because they do not have to spend the great amount of energy it takes to resist racism. Sexist factors affecting them are minimal and they can spend more time acquiring material resources.

Chicano men do not live as long as white men. Chicano men die earlier because of inadequate health care and the added stresses imposed by racism and sexism. Anglos, especially Anglo women, are not to the same degree nor in the same manner as Chicanos subjected to this victimization—and the shortening of life expectancies and decrease in life chances. Further study of mortality rates is certainly required, perhaps beginning with the data collected by the U.S. Department of the Census (1985).

REVIEW OF THE MULTISEGMENTED SOCIAL VALUE SYSTEMS

Members of the Chicano community and Chicano scholars (Acuna, 1988; Barrera, 1979; Muñoz, 1972) have recognized a dual social system for almost two centuries. Since before 1848, Chicanos have recognized that there is a set of laws and unwritten rules for Anglos and another set of rules and laws for Chicanos and other people of color. A third set of laws and rules exists for women. In the case of the American Chicana this perspective should be extended to include her in at least three value systems: one for women, one for the poor, and one for people of color. If individuals fall into any combination of these categories, their life chances decrease. Added dimensions, like lesbianism or mental or physical limitations, further decrease upward mobility in U.S. society and further decrease life expectancy and opportunities.

On the surface all Americans are equal but in reality people of color and women have a second- or third-place standing. Women of color often make up the least-valued segment in a multisegmented social system that operates on numerous levels. The levels include different rules, expectations, and positions of status, power, and prestige for Anglo men, Anglo women, the poor, men of color, women of color, poor men of color, and poor women of color. Specific jobs, social opportunities, and legal protections are available to each, but they are all more available to those with higher status, higher prestige, and higher value or social worth (Reiss et al., 1961).

The multisegmented system and the privilege it offers to the elite can also be seen clearly at work in the criminal justice system. Being a person of color means increased chances of encountering the law, being sent to prison, and appearing on death row, especially if a white, Anglo male has been killed. Wealthy Anglos will have fewer of these experiences. When they make contact with law officials the reason for contact and duration of the experience will be different. The poorer person, generally, has an experience as a suspect or as an offender, rather than as a person needing protection, information, or assistance.

The National Association for the Advancement of Colored People (NAACP) has documented that the poor and people of color receive more guilty verdicts, longer sentences, and higher fines in the criminal justice system. More people of color go to jail. These findings are directly dependent on at least three factors: the money a person has to hire a competent attorney; the network of influential persons that can assist the individual; and what that person represents to the establishment, the social value and worth of the individual or the social group the individual represents.

Chicanas feel the need to make corrections in the criminal justice system. They look toward those that govern the United States to accomplish this. Many people of color do not trust the government to address their concerns, and some do not view government officials as a body that has final responsibility for social decisions. The will of the common people should be allowed to govern. The belief in nonresponsive government is based upon experiences in Chicano history, the violation of the Treaty of Guadalupe Hidalgo and how the government has formulated racist, sexist policies that negatively affect Chicanos, people of color, and the people of other Spanish-speaking and Third World countries. Yet, while some Chicanos are skeptical, others believe in the current governing structure and in the possibility of legislating a policy on the dissolution of racism and sexism.

Racism and sexism have become American cultural characteristics. They are embedded in the social fabric. Change in the ingrained social stratification system has to be approached from within the social institutions simultaneously. It has to be integrated into family lifestyle, religion, politics, education, the law, the health system, and economics. The truth is, of course, that many people gain from social stratification and many people silently support multisegmentation. Society has put much time and energy into denying that social stratification exists; but it does exist, and the study of minority women has assisted social scientists in understanding this more fully.

REFERENCES

Acuna, Rodolfo. 1988. *Occupied America: A History of Chicanos* (3rd ed.). New York: Harper & Row.

Barrera, Mario. 1979. *Race and Class in the Southwest.* South Bend, Ind.: University of Notre Dame Press.

Benson, Margaret. 1969. "The Political Economy of Women's Liberation." *Monthly Review*, Vol. 21, No. 4 (September): 37.

______. 1981. "An Analysis of Mexican-American Homemaking." Unpublished paper presented at 1977 National Association of Chicano Studies Conference, Claremont, California.

Engels, Frederick, ed. 1967. *Capital: A Critical Analysis of Capitalist Production*, Vol. 1. New York: International Publishers.

______. *Capital: The Process of Circulation of Capital*, Vol. 2.

______. *Capital: The Process of Capitalist Production*, Vol. 3.

Garcia, Mario. 1981. *Desert Immigrant: The Mexicans of El Paso, 1880-1920.* New Haven, Conn.: Yale University Press.

Gerth, H. H., and C. Wright Mills. 1946. *From Max Weber: Essays in Sociology*. New York: Oxford University Press.

Harrington, Michael. 1963. *The Other American: Poverty in the United States.* Baltimore: Penguin Books.

Kiev, Aria. 1968. *Curanderismo: Mexican American Folk Psychiatry.* New York: Free Press.

Melville, Margaritta B. 1980. *Twice a Minority*. St. Louis, Mo.: Mosby Press.

Mirande, Alfredo. 1985. *The Chicano Experience.* South Bend, Ind.: University of Notre Dame Press.

Muñoz, Carlos, Jr. 1972. *The Politics of Urban Protest: A Model of Political Analysis.* Ph.D. dissertation, Claremont, California, Graduate School of Government.

Reiss, Albert J., O. D. Duncan, Paul K. Hatt, and C. C. North. 1961. *Occupations and Social Status*. Glencoe, Ill.: Free Press.

Rose, Peter. 1981. *They and We: Racial and Ethnic Relations in the United States* (3rd ed.). New York: Random House.

Terkel, Studs. 1974. *Working*. New York: Pantheon Books.

United States Bureau of the Census. 1985. "Persons of Spanish Origin in the United States." Current Population Reports Series. No. 310 (July): 20; No. 328 (August). Washington, D.C.: GPO.

Chapter 10

New Directions in Chicana Feminist Theory and Practice

This chapter surveys the direction of social change and theorizes about the lives of Chicanas at the national and the international levels. Some emphasis is upon the social sciences, but topics of concentration include lesbian Chicanas, the role of women in the politics of the Catholic church, and the role of the church in the lives and politics of Chicano people. A theoretical perspective becomes important because of the number of U.S. Hispanics and Hispanic Catholics, and because the notion of liberation is growing stronger among church activists and in the community as a whole.

The focus in this chapter is on liberation theology and war—men making it, women and children enduring it. The Chicana's role in liberation, the curtailment of war, and the resulting oppression of people are presented as an effort to link theory and practice in the United States, Central America, and Latin America. Akin to this is the discussion on the political use of academic scholarship and the inequalities found in academia and its administration.

I have related that dominant U.S. perspectives, realities, and depictions of Chicanas have been tainted by the biased perceptions of a Eurocentric, Anglo, and male-dominated point of view. The few Anglo-dominant women who have written or conducted research on Chicanas have used white, Anglo, male-dominated paradigms. From this, the United States has inherited the myth of an innocent history and a cultural inferiority complex. Most Americans believe that the United States has an almost spotless history in the defense of the mission to spread and protect democracy at all costs. This is a contention whereby the blemishes of war, imperialism, and colonialism are hidden and disguised. Examples of these are plentiful and have been cited throughout this work.

These conscious and/or unconscious efforts to disguise history make it appear as if males were the only beings who had done anything important. Because dominant Anglo culture works in dichotomies, since men are important, their counterparts, women, especially women of color, appear unimportant. Relegating a population to this status makes it easier to continue to abuse and discount people of color.

THE USE OF ACADEMIA AND THE GROWTH OF KNOWLEDGE

Chicana feminist theory has been dominated by the class-biased socialist feminist position which erases gender, race, and ethnicity. This position conceptualizes women and racial/ethnic minorities as workers, bland members of the working class, oppressed by the ruling capitalist elite. Capitalism has been destructive to the Chicana. It has forced her into accepting her own oppression by accepting a male-dominant society. This acceptance has limited the Chicano people's liberation by making many of them homophobic. Critics of the Marxist, socialist perspective note that not only does it not allow for a discussion on racism, color, and gender, but it allows only minimal hope of escape from oppression and a move toward equality via revolution. From a Marxist, socialist perspective revolution cannot take place unless all the oppressed recognize their common oppression. For some Chicana feminists, lesbians included, this is taking too long.

Emma Perez extends this argument to assert that during and after the revolution men refuse to give up their power (1990b). They refuse to give up power at the expense of women's sanity. This text has discussed abusive relationships. It should be added that when women voice their oppression and/or act out their discontent, men attempt to make them appear foolish, deviant, or mentally ill in order to perpetuate female social instability. Examples of Chicanas who resist this analysis and support male dominance are easy to find within Chicano communities. A natural question is: Why would Chicanas resist Chicana feminism? They do so because they refuse to acknowledge that the men make the rules in their society. In addition, they are addicted to the denigration and abuse of male-dominated capitalism. This addiction to capitalism does not allow them to recognize their own oppression.

Chicanas also do not fit into the socialist paradigm because white socialist feminists have not dealt effectively with their racism. Those doing biased research have been confronted, but they continue to overlook the sustaining social, cultural, and spiritual components inherent to the Chicana way of life that will not allow the acceptance of an understanding of themselves as inferior.

The resulting biased paradigms of traditional social scientists have not only harmed La Chicana, they have misguided American social science in the United States and have denied American social science an international leadership role by imposing a much too narrow scope on how discrimination functions.

The truth is that oppression by means of discrimination is based on various factors, among which are gender, sexuality, and sexual orientation. These are variables generally treated separately, but in fact they intersect. They reflect the well-documented fact that men refuse to give power to women and to those who choose to be sexual with members of their own gender.

Chicana feminist theory examines the cultural structure to expand upon the nature of patriarchy. It expands upon the internal colonial model and the calls for decolonization, liberation from Eurocentric philosophies and ways of life. However, the largest step forward in developing an alternative paradigm is inherent in the work of Chicana lesbians, who have incorporated major contributions from Chicana feminists in an analysis of the lesbian woman's experience in the United States. There exists now sufficient knowledge to move toward a paradigm shift, a change in the broad way of thinking, that promotes a strategy for social change in the development of conscious cultural restructuring. To do this one should focus upon sexuality.

The issues and phobias, especially those about lesbians, that have plagued academics are but symptoms of the forces that shape the cultural structure that gives shape to cultural identification. The manifestation of phobias in academia is not surprising, but it needs to be addressed and remedied. The best way to do this is to take an intimate look at what shapes the human experience. Such an in-depth look reveals that sexuality is the most intimate human knowledge. For Chicana lesbians, it is the most intimate knowledge of sexual and gender oppression.

General academic knowledge about culture, sexuality, and gender has concentrated upon matriarchal and patriarchal cultures. Cultures have been analyzed as tracing inheritance along either the mother's female side of the family or the father's male side of the family. There is no paradigm for people who do not wish to trace inheritance or who choose another cultural pattern. In the case of Chicano culture, scholars have first documented the patriarchal side; then feeble attempts have been made to trace the matriarchal side. This can be seen in the twenty-year developmental program of Chicano studies. First men, and a few women, criticized Anglo work; then Chicanas revealed the sexism in the work of their male counterparts, and finally there was a movement to identify Chicano women as Chicanas. It was not until 1990 at the National Association of Chicano Studies annual conference that Chicana feminists and Chicana lesbians began to talk about sexual oppression, sexuality, and their impact on Chicana feminist theory. This was a major step forward in promoting a paradigm shift, a move away from the side-by-side hierarchal thinking of patriarchy and matriarchy. It was a move toward a holistic approach to theory construction.

For a few this shift promoted conscious social change that recognized the internalization of the superiority of dominant male-identified males, male-identified females, female-identified males, and female-identified females who knowingly or unknowingly support a hierarchal structure. The Chicana feminists who have managed to change their lives and their academic perspectives have at best internalized identifications of themselves as female-identified females and still live with a fear of homosexuality and lesbianism.

This fear, homophobia, is rooted in patriarchal and matriarchal cultural perspectives. In the search for liberty and egalitarianism, one must look at the cultural structure and its role in promoting oppression. This is most clear in a marital or love relationship, where individuals will establish relationships as long as they come from compatible structures. Core social values guide whom people choose as lovers and direct people to desire what is socially acceptable. Internalization of these values limits the potential for protest and revolution and has given Chicana lesbians problems with Anglo male- and female-identified feminists (Perez, 1990b).

Chicana feminist problems with Anglo feminists go beyond white racism. Basic to this is gender identify fixation and whether or not white feminists have escaped the hierarchal trappings of both patriarchy and matriarchy as it is known in dominant America. Patriarchally identified females and males will cooperate as long as they play their roles the way the cultural structure produces them. If that structure is disrupted, as it was with the feminist movement, the relationships will change and/or the group will restructure again, with or without a patriarchal format. For the most part, white feminists have restructured within the already defined formats. They restructured along patriarchal or matriarchal lines. It is therefore not uncommon to find Anglo women who act like men and Chicanas who act like white women who act like men.

The same is true of the new American matriarchal-structured culture. This culture is an alternative only to the degree that it is not patriarchal. However, it is socially stratified just as rigidly as patriarchy and the social consequences are just as severe if identification is not matriarchal. This model, it must be noted, does not analyze Native American culture, a culture worthwhile to our study as we seek alternative lifestyles with more liberty.

There can be real trouble in relationship formation, be it personal or academic, when a matriarchally identified person relates to a patriarchally identified person, either male or female. Power struggles and misunderstandings ensue. The ability to communicate is often conflictual, and both sides want the other to think as they do and/or, in the case of love relationships, take care of them.

Patriarchy demands that men be macho but that they also be female dependent. They are socialized to have women take care of them. In dominant matriarchal culture women are socialized to take care of themselves and to choose whether or not to take care of men. Chicana feminists want neither of these structures. They want an interdependent culture similar to what they had before the Anglos' arrival. But, as has been related in a previous chapter, this culture was disrupted by U.S. colonization.

After colonization, Chicano culture has struggled to restructure. Colonization under U.S. oppression cannot tolerate this culture to restructure under its old gender-balanced format. The gender-balanced format is threatening because it is inconsistent with patriarchy and other stratified structures. The dominant culture can tolerate restructuring only under patriarchal lines and severely punishes those who do not conform. Radical lesbian Chicana feminists have felt the social blows of this intolerance as they have experienced alienation from the dominant and Chicano cultures, from Anglo feminists, and from Chicana feminists.

Under colonization the cultural structure of Chicanos appears to be radically changed. It is not. It is in flux. It has gone through Eurocentric patriarchal restructuring to produce for a short period a hierarchal system dominated by men. In the 1960s Chicana feminists challenged this cultural structure. They sought a gender balance. In building a new cultural structure the strategy for some has been to identify with indigenous people, who also are colonized. The most recent move is toward more liberation by creating a new alternative, a culture that recognizes and respects humanity, that is androgynous and not stratified.

The social sciences go beyond creating theories and paradigms that explain what happens to people in a society. They are taught to the ruling elite and their followers and have social and political use. Social science research has been used to legitimize opinion, formulate public policy, and provide funding for a variety of social service programs. In the 1960s the social sciences were used to gain an understanding of civil discontent in various factions of the society.

Social scientists in the United States have proceeded in their science as if dominant cultural social facts were general and universal. They have done this without considering the various cultural manifestations, the structure and function of discrimination, and the imposition of public policies formulated by the dominant group to control populations of color. The function of this control has been to create the appearance of a homogenous society accepting of dominant rule. The Chicana has had to develop her analysis within and outside of this appearance. She has done it by linking theory to practice, practice to theory. This has been her greatest contribution to society and the social sciences. Her analysis is grounded in the realities of her life from an inside-outside perspective.

AN INTERNATIONAL PERSPECTIVE

In *Toward a Chicano Social Science* (1988), which looks at old paradigms and building new paradigms, I argue that La Chicana (and women in general) have developed lateral thinking—that is, alternative ways of thinking and organizing—that are not always consistent with Anglo male ways of thinking and doing things. This has happened because they have functioned with oppression at many levels. If given serious attention, this experience can produce developments toward new paradigms that can be used to create a more just society. The problem, of course, has been that the dominant society believes that Chicanas have nothing to teach.

The Chicano movement and the events leading up to it were instrumental in building a new paradigm. Given the conditions under which Chicanas have had to live, the Chicana feminist civil rights movement was bound to happen, and the above analysis was bound to develop. But it could happen only if something kept the human spirit alive long enough to write about it. What kept this spirit alive was the women of this culture who would not forget that there was another way to live.

This other way to live includes a Third World perspective on the idea of liberation. Chicanos have witnessed the creations and reactions of oppressed people in Third World (note that I still feel the term is elitist) countries. A Third World perspective in the Chicano community evolved before general knowledge about U.S. involvements in these countries was widespread. It evolved because Chicanos experienced social oppression, the mighty power and control of the dominant society, and because some Chicano people would not accept oppressive conditions. Resistance, ethnicity, continues because social oppression continues. It functions to make the group cohesive.

There is a complex interconnection combining women's economic exploitation with their patriarchal and racial oppression. Sylvia Lizarraga (1988) explains that the fundamental differences between the feminism of Third World women and that of middle-class white women in the United States is that the struggle for emancipation by Third World women has been defined historically not only as one against patriarchal ideology but also as a simultaneous, ongoing struggle against economic exploitation and sociopolitical oppression. Even though the theoretical formulations posited by social feminists in the United States provide the foundations for the analysis of capitalist patriarchy, these have not yet provided for a complete analysis of a combined oppression based on class, race, and gender. This combination is the kind of Third World exploitation experienced by women of color in this country and explains why women of color have not complained when analyzed under the elitist label.

It suffices to say that when a society is thus characterized, it sets up conditions for social reform and revolution. Social reform and revolution reek of violence. Chicanas have demanded and taken viable steps in nonviolent social reform. The majority, however, have bypassed revolution and have sought to participate in the ongoing social structure, not to destroy it and replace it, but to expand it through their participation.

Factors contributing to the slow movement toward new paradigms is inherent in the nature of oppression. Powerless people need power and control over their own lives.They formulate different ideologies in order to do this, but they can also do this when the population is large and there is a cultural network of support. Differences among the population fragments the social movement. It is thus in the dominant power's interest to sustain differences among minority populations. This is especially easy in competitive cultures, or when the oppressed have internalized the values of the oppressor. Resistance becomes a social force when the oppressed can no longer tolerate social conditions.

In spite of ideological differences among Chicanas, the work of La Chicana is gaining national and even international importance. Chicanas are part of political and academic dialogues in Mexico, Central and Latin

America, Spain, France, and Germany. Foreign scholars have discovered the academic contributions of Chicanas before U.S. scholars. The 1990 Hispanics in the Americas conference was hosted by academicians in Germany. Its theme was the nature of Chicana feminism. France and Spain have also hosted conferences where the issues and contributions of La Chicana have been discussed.

In other spheres this author has engaged in international Chicano-Jewish dialogues and political and cultural exchange trips. Mexican feminists and Chicana feminists are in frequent contact. There is also dialogue with international women among national board members of Young Women's Christian Association (YWCA) of the United States. However, Chicanas here have had problems with Anglo women who want to dominate the organization.

REFORM AND REVOLUTION AS MODELS OF SOCIAL CHANGE THEORY

Because of the large number of women in this country and because of the country's cultural diversity, it is not reasonable to expect a feminist consciousness to evolve at the same time for all women. But a review of the literature on Chicanas reveals that the internal colonial model, already discussed, is the leading theoretical model in Chicano and Chicana studies. Basically, it is a good model. It accounts for social-historical discrimination; it also explains why Chicanos have not been assimilated into the dominant culture and lays the groundwork for social change by calling for decolonization. One of the drawbacks of the model is that it does not outline the kind of social change that should take place, or how to bring about that change.

The internal colonial model is an extension of work by Albert Memmi (1965) and Franz Fannon (1963). An essential characteristic of the model is the violent situation in which an outside group dominates and exploits an indigenous group by justifying its actions as good for the colonized population. A mythology is essential, for it allows the colonizer and the colonized to internalize the colonizer as a superior agent of civilization. This supports the redefinition of the colonized as inferior, being too emotional, not able to engage in logical thinking, being fatalistic, and being unable to control their own lives.

From this emerges a variety of attitudes, including those of members of the colonized group who are against their own group: Anti-Chicana Chicanas do exist. These women accept the colonizer's view of themselves and their people and identify with the oppressor. There are also other reactions. The antigroup member may feel she is the exception to the colonizer's version of what her people represent. The feeling is that all Chicanas are the way the colonizer says they are except her because she has "made it," or somehow she has escaped the trappings of minority status. Those with this ideology overlook the fact that the colonizer allows those who most resemble the colonizer to appear to "succeed" only if the colonized member accepts their definition of success. Frequently, this means giving up indigenous culture.

Another reaction to colonization is that the colonized may feel that some of what is said by the colonizer is true, but may still be proud of being a member of the colonized group. There is nothing wrong with the ways of the colonized. A final reaction is that the colonized feel the colonizer's view of them is true only because the conditions under which they have had to live have shaped that truth. It is at this point that the colonizer is in trouble because this ideology gives rise to a liberation movement. Chicanas have come to this realization.

As long as the colonized do not realize this, they can be controlled. Systematic control through discrimination is an essential feature of the internal colonial model: populations are controlled within the boundaries of the larger country. The Chicana's internal colonial experience as a member of a minority population comprises a Third World within the boundaries of the United States. The Chicana relationship to the dominant culture is involuntary and results in the minority population being labeled, discredited, and relegated to a status of inferiority by the colonizer. The minority or colony is internal if the population has the same formal status as any other group, but in reality (informally) it is oppressed and subjugated to secondary citizenship.

Revolution and reform appear to be the two leading alternatives for those seeking change. Reform via their participation in the ongoing social structure appears to be the form of social change most frequently chosen by Chicanas. There have always been those women who wanted revolution, an entirely different structure. They have sought to overthrow the colonizer violently or nonviolently and create a new society.

LIBERATION THEOLOGY AS A SOCIAL CHANGE THEORY

Attempts at reform have taken place in several social institutions. One structure in which this has taken place is the Catholic church. Only a few Chicanos have openly called for an entirely different religious structure. Those who have chosen to work within the Catholic church have focused upon liberation theology as a reformist ideological framework for social change. Liberation theology has, however, primarily remained active as a social change theory among those who work within the church. Those not active in the church have paid little attention to liberation theology because of the political separation of church and state in the United States and because to some degree it has been suppressed by church officials.

The relief of oppression is the focus of two important holidays that incorporate religion: el Cinco de Mayo, the fifth of May, and el Dieciséis de Septiembre, the sixteenth of September. These are days of prayer and celebration of Mexico's independence and the search for peaceful existence. Ironically, these are also days when Chicano gatherings have encountered police conflict and surveillance. Recently these days have proven to be days of peaceful celebration of ethnicity. Perhaps the dominant society is less threatened by ethnic celebrations of an oppressed group; or perhaps the oppressed groups have demonstrated that they have internalized their oppression and thus the calls for struggle, for liberation, are less frequent.

In its attempt to change, the Catholic church has acknowledged these days. Some feel their acknowledgment has been tokenism; others feel it has been significant. A call for more significant social change through liberation theology has been introduced to the Chicano community by means of the highlighted debates in Central and Latin America, where priests and church members have striven to make real in practice the theories governing Christianity. Activists seek to get the world power of the Catholic church involved in lifting political oppression among its people.

A theology of liberation emphasizes that personal and institutional oppression must be eliminated as an aspect of spiritual salvation. The institutional church has emphasized a more narrow conception of spirituality and salvation. It emphasizes salvation of the individual soul (Mosqueda, 1986). Fundamentally, the theology of liberation attempts to link the church and society as interrelated phenomena that simultaneously promote civil rights as inherent in the teachings of the gospel. In a theology of liberation there is no dichotomy between spiritual and temporal existence. Eternal salvation is linked to secular liberation.

Adherents of liberation theology note that there is a role in liberation theology for La Chicana as a member of her oppressed population (Isasi-Díaz and Tarango, 1988). Others disagree, claiming that no gender roles or dichotomies exist. Focus is upon the empowerment of communities through Christian salvation. Little mention has been made in Chicano circles of the fact that Christianity is the religion of the Spanish colonizer; that European colonization imposed this religion on native people; that

U.S. colonization persecuted Mexican-American Catholics and indigenous religion, and that it controls them to this very day.

The definition of Christianity, then, becomes an issue. Feminist nuns hurl charges that Christianity is male-dominated and male-biased. They cite that only men can be priests and only a male can become pope. They truly do not believe that God meant to differentiate between the sexes. In addition, Christian behavior has had its own contradictions, and these contradictions have been founded in the politics of men.

Yet in the area of religion and spirituality, women becoming priests or other members of the clergy does not appear to be the urgent issue for Chicanas that it was for Anglo feminists in other religions. Males adhering to liberation theology have very little to say about women becoming priests. Chicano women and men have struggled within the church to make it more responsive to Chicano concerns by basing their arguments on the need for viable participation in ongoing religious rites, more direct services for Chicano poor, and more priests. Only a few have voiced a need for women to become priests, and only a few have emerged to question and confront the power of the pope.

My own research in Bessemer (1990) found that in protest to the Catholic church's resistance, many Chicanos have converted to other religions, some of which are highly fundamental. The most frequently cited reason for conversion is contradictions in the Catholic church's theology. Other reasons include the church's overuse of ceremony and ritual and the heavy role the priests play. The latter keeps individuals from forming and maintaining a direct relationship with God. The priests and the church structure also interfere too much with what people want to do. For example, services are not in Spanish and there is a lack of Spanish music.

In contrast, the fundamentalist religions hold entire services in Spanish. They have Spanish prayers, teachings, and songs. People are an integral participatory part of the services, not just the audience. The new religions are also more expressive than the Catholic religion. People can, for instance, testify before the group. They can ask questions, clap hands to music, cry and pray out loud with much dancing and joy in knowing that the Lord exists. People offer to pray for one another. They ask for prayer and they touch and visit one another. In alternative churches, women have found new roles and new power. There they are called sisters and the men are their brothers. Little or no hierarchy exists. Women testify at microphones, they lead prayers, preach, cite passages from the Bible, sing, and generally take a fuller part in the services. In the non-Catholic churches, sociopolitical awareness is manifested in speeches called testimonies, which are unlike anything in the Catholic church's practice. Testimonies, however, rarely lead to action.

THE FUNCTION OF RELIGION IN BUILDING IDEOLOGY

A sociological definition of religion extends that religion is a social institution. Social institutions shape ideology, for they are social structures built around widely shared and accepted beliefs, procedures, norms, and values. In addition, social institutions endure because they meet the needs of people. They are slow to change and are linked to other institutions that support them and assist them in guiding human behavior. Religion as a social institution is linked to the family, economics, politics, and the health delivery system. This intersection functions to maintain the status quo. Minority status has worked to keep most Catholic Chicanos wanting change, but not too radical a change. In summary there is social pressure upon Chicanos to conform to the belief system supported by their culture and their oppression.

Emile Durkheim (1915) wrote an entire volume on how religion is necessary for a society because it integrates values. This crucial factor sustains social cohesion and social control. This factor explains why the Chicano people and society in general continue to internalize dominant perspectives. Catholic doctrine is passively accepted to give direction to Chicano life, thus functioning in Chicano culture as it does in the dominant culture.

Chicana spirituality does not always mean organized religion. Rather, it is a fundamental belief about the nature of the material and intangible world with indigenous (part Indian) characteristics. An example of an indigenous characteristic is that some Chicanos believe that the spirit of ancestors can guide them in this life. Chicanas sometimes say that the U.S. Anglo has become spiritually void. In having internalized some American values, some Chicanos have also lost spirituality, especially indigenous elements.

Religious spirituality contributes to ideology. Dominant religion and the ideology it shapes tell social participants that social arrangements are adequate, that they are how they should be: natural. For the most part, ideologies become cemented as part of the socialization process, which does not end. A person continues learning social roles, norms, and behaviors through the life cycle. Ideologies can change, but unless individuals have an intense desire to change or a significant event occurs, most people never think about what they have learned by being a social participant. They take their knowledge for granted as actual, as truth. For a great number of individuals the social structure upholds their beliefs. Thus, they have little motivation to change, and they may live with a false consciousness, believing that what they believe is true.

Like other people, Chicanas do not think much about their own church history and the nature of the historical roots of their faith. Some are unaware of their indigenous spiritual ancestors, for they have dissasociated, come to feel ashamed of being Indian, and do not claim indigenous heritage.

Chicano religion and spirituality is a system of shared beliefs and practices built around the idea of natural and supernatural forces that link the individual to a much greater power. Some of these beliefs and practices are indigenous. Chicanos, like other people, use supernatural forces as an explanation for that which is known and that which is unknown. Characteristic of the manifestation of religion is the notion of god or gods, the nature of the spirit life, the afterlife, and salvation and damnation. For Chicanas this involves prayer and ritual of a physical, psychological, and spiritual nature.

But what else affects religion and spirituality? For La Chicana it is the relationships of individuals to their god. Religion and spirituality assist in defining the Chicana in relationship to earth, heaven, hell, and purgatory; to other supernatural beings like the saints; and to living and dead relatives. La Chicana's god manifests itself in every element of her communal life. Her spiritual relationship is exercised when she studies in college in order to return to her barrio to help her people. It manifests itself when she bathes her children. However, other influences intervene when status, power, and prestige are bestowed upon her—or, more frequently, not bestowed upon her—for they are given in differential amounts as social rewards for conformity to the dominant group.

Religion and spirituality have helped Chicanas understand their place in the universe. All too frequently intervening manmade variables, as discussed in this text, have placed her in an adverse or secondary relationship to other groups of people, especially to Anglo men. This means that there is social space between her and others. This social space has assisted in making her accept being poorer, having lower status, power, and prestige; but it has also assisted in sustaining the ideology of liberation.

Feminist Chicanas are aware of oppressive social forces; few have chosen to struggle against them. From birth they have lived with Catholicism and have come to know its highly bureaucratic nature. In the 1960s and 1970s they recognized that Catholicism was frequently consistent with real dominant norms and values. Hierarchical positions are held by men; areas of specialization are defined and administered by men. Official creeds and formal training required for participation in this sphere are also defined and administered by men. Even when women dominate an area, such as the recruitment, training, and mentoring of nuns, the fundamental theology is dictated by men.

Blea (1990) confirms the male-dominated stance of the church. In addition, I found that although a great number of people said they were Catholic, they did not always practice their religion by going to church every Sunday and holy days of obligation, saying daily prayers, receiving holy communion, or otherwise behaving as Catholics. They also had indigenous practices that followed the life cycle. They baptized children and got married and were buried in the Catholic church. Some people had home altars and images of the saints. They used their Catholic religion at the same time they used Indian herbs, prayer, and medicine. Those who had chosen to attend church and fully live Catholic lives sought to make Catholicism more relevant to themselves by having music, prayers, and readings in Spanish. And in the religious festivals Chicano Catholics included a variety of Indian food. (Note that until very recently Catholic doctrine historically excluded indigenous practices and even interpreted them as unsophisticated, the work of the uncivilized, and even as the work of the devil.)

Yet indigenous culture has contributed much to the Mexican-American and American way of life. For the Chicano the relationship between food and spirituality is a close one. Mexican food, always present at celebrations, has been greatly influenced by indigenous culture. Traditionally, this has been a women's domain and an essential one at that, since humans cannot live without food. Its production, preparation, and storage are of utmost necessity. Heriberto Garcia Rivas, author of *Cocina Pre-Hispánica Mexicana* (1988), maintains that the interchange of food between Indians and Spanish Europeans created a "cocina mestiza," a combination of indigenous food prepared in a Spanish style or European ingredients prepared in an indigenous style.

These cross-cultural productions include spirituality; cooking utensils such as the *metate, molcajete,* and *comal*, which are used for grinding and mixing; certain flavors, such as vanilla and chocolate; and condiments. Culinary contributions include the preparation of chile, squash, avocados, beans, potatoes, and spinach. Corn began in Indian kitchens, as did certain meats like venison. Beverages included cacao, plus a variety of fruit drinks and juices, liquors (*pulque*), fish, fruits (papaya, pineapple, bananas), herbs, mushrooms, cacti, and seeds and nuts. When combined, these ingredients produce *tamales, tostadas, tacos, tortillas,* stews, soups, salads, and roasts, which produce an attractive festival of color. Tortilla is frequently used as the host during Catholic communion.

The vibrant colors of indigenous cuisine sustained the conquistadors and the women and children who came with them and after them. The Spanish brought, for example, goats, wheat, and fruit trees (peaches, pears, cherries, apples). To facilitate labor and travel, they also brought the horse and oxen. They brought cows, pigs, and chickens. These items were blessed by the priests who also traveled to the New World. The long history of the food and how Chicanos relate to food has assisted in building an ideology.

Many of these foods and herbs were used for healing purposes. Health and healing were not separated from spirituality. Combined with Indian food and medical traditions, they produced a working health and healing system that, when integrated with Indian and Catholic religious practices and beliefs, became a way of life. The study of La Chicana has taught the nation that it is possible to live in harmony with people of other cultures, for even though painful, Indians and Chicanos have done this in learning to live with each other. From Southwest Chicanas society at large can learn of the integrated Indian and Spanish traditions of childrearing, *Penitentes* (a spiritual community), la Virgin de Guadalupe (the Virgin Mary), *brujería* (frequently referred to as a witch), and *curanderísmo, baptísmo* (baptism), *confirmación* (confirmation), and beliefs in La Llorona (the crying woman), ghosts, or spirits. Their complex system of health and healing, belief in the supernatural, good and evil as elements of religion—all constitute for the Chicana a world view somewhat consistent yet different from that of the Anglo American. All this must be a consideration of those wishing to produce theories that explain the life of La Chicana.

Increasingly, this knowledge has been violated, discredited, challenged, diluted, separated, and channeled into institutions rooted in the dominant society that vulgarizes it. This vulgarization must be considered when constructing a social change theory of an oppressed population. A new social change theory must include a recipe for direction and quality of change, or it is but an empty mental exercise, producing nothing of value for society.

CHICANA CONTRIBUTIONS TO SOCIAL CHANGE THEORY

The analysis of Chicanas in the United States has taught the world that some populations of American women are bicultural and that Chicanas can and do have strong roles in their culture. Chicanas give definition to cultural values, norms, and communicative symbols. They are nurturing and supportive not only of their young but also of their society as a whole through times of crisis.

The study of La Chicana has also taught that culture will sustain itself in spite of oppression; that it plays a role in political resistance. In fact, oppression assists in sustaining Chicano cultural integrity through some violent history in this country. Another lesson to be learned is that the oppressed must remain conscious of the direction of the change they seek. Theoretically speaking, from Chicano studies we have learned that theories of Chicano oppression need to extend themselves beyond explaining how and why a group was conquered to suggesting how to become liberated; but this is how theories expand. They extend certain premises. They are critiqued and criticized, accepted or rejected, and amended.

How a group becomes oppressed includes several components or phases. First, any heroic figures, deeds, and contributions the group possesses or can lay claim to must be degraded, demeaned, and destroyed. There is a dehumanizing component: Human worth must be extracted from the population. Sexist jokes have functioned to dehumanize Chicanas, for example. The language must be prohibited, made fun of, and eradicated because ideological and cultural behavior is consistent with the structure and function, or the use, of language. There is, for example, a movement against the use of such words as *liberation, oppression, colonization*, and *revolution*, words now frequently associated with an outdated historical period, the 1960s. No longer in vogue, these words have never been palatable to sections of the population. For the truth is that these words threaten those with highly internalized dominant values. Indeed, essential in colonizing is the internalization of the dominant values by the oppressed to the point where the oppressor needs to do very little. The oppressed will oppress themselves once they have internalized dominant values. Keep in mind that the dominant group will never accept the oppressed group into its ranks until it becomes just like them, mentally, physically, and spiritually.

The question remains: What is liberation? Chicano liberation is not the individualistic internalization of dominant values and joining the mainstream. Chicana liberation has meant freedom, emancipation from racism and sexism, plus cultural sovereignty: that the cultural integrity and dignity of a people be recognized and respected as equal to any other. Chicanos have demanded that the authority of the Treaty of Guadalupe Hidalgo be recognized, that they be incorporated as viable participants directing the American way of life. Liberation for most

Chicanos has not included supremacy or jurisdiction of a racist-sexist history.

Social scientists and others can learn more about struggles for liberation by noting that in the case of La Chicana, ideological development has not been consistent. This is rooted in the heterogeneous nature of the group, the degree of urbanization, and the internalization of dominant social values. Lack of homogeneity causes fragmentation and assists in maintaining oppression at the same time it gives individuals freedom. But is individual freedom more important than the freedom of an entire group of people? The Chicana says no.

The analysis of La Chicana has also taught the world that people do not forget easily. And when they do finally forget, society possesses half-understood remnants of their history. People lose track of why they do some things. They relegate some practices to the arena of tradition. Thus, sometimes there is a lag between what is known and what is done.

PERSONAL POLITICAL ACTS

For Chicana activists the struggle toward liberation is a lifestyle. Most of what they do, even marriage, is a political act. As do most Americans, Chicanas generally marry within their own race. When a political consciousness exists, however, this is done on purpose. There is also pressure inside and outside Chicano culture to marry within the same ethnic group. Most people still frown upon intermarriage.

In the United States a social premise is that people marry primarily because they fall in love. What attracts them, however, is strongly dictated by the norms and roles of culture. Our society strongly influences individuals to marry people like themselves. Of course, in some families the message differs: Women are supposed to marry "up." Love as a basis of marriage is a relatively new idea, and our society remains tied to a time when marriage was arranged on the basis of landholdings and the need for power, status, and prestige. Few people today would admit that they marry for reasons other than love, and many use love as justification, to mask other motives.

From a theoretical perspective, the workings of racism, sexism, and the idea of liberation as a lifestyle may be seen more clearly when we observe intermarriage. Given that U.S. society attributes varying degrees of social worth to different social groups, the most valued and powerful social group is the dominant group: the white group commonly referred to as Anglos. The most valued and powerful persons in society are white Anglo men, followed by white females. Men of color are less valued than white females, while minority females of color are the least valued of all.

Thus, when a white man marries, he maintains his position of power because his wife, as a woman, is less socially valued. When a minority man marries, he also maintains a position of power, particularly in choosing a minority female, for he sees her as not his equal. However, he may choose to marry a white Anglo female in order to feel he is marrying up because white Anglo women have a higher social ranking than do minority men. This social manipulation does not grant the minority male any more power, but it does give him the delusion of being empowered.

When white women decide to marry, they, like minority men, have a choice. They can marry up by marrying a white Anglo male, remaining in a secondary position to their husbands, or they can marry down on the racial scale and be more powerful by marrying a minority male. The Chicana also has a choice. She is at the lower end of the social racial-sexual scale and can marry up by marrying a white Anglo male. She also can marry down to maintain some power by marrying a black male. In addition, she can marry laterally by marrying a Chicano.

For the sake of cultural continuity and solidarity in the struggle for liberation, some Chicanas choose to marry Chicanos. This model, of course, excludes homosexual relationships and looks only at heterosexual relationships. Research into the nature of interracial homosexual and lesbian relationships is certainly warranted. To a certain degree the issue is addressed in *Chicana Lesbians: The Girls Our Mothers Warned Us About* (1991). This issue of Third Woman Press consists of groundbreaking work done by Chicana lesbian writers. All those involved—the writers, editor Carla Trujillo, Norma Alarcon, and other members of Third Woman Press—are to be commended for contributing significantly to the study of La Chicana.

Because white Anglo males have received many social rewards on the basis of their whiteness and their maleness, women have had to learn to live and create in a secondary position. Sometimes women engage in male-female relationships in ways that are not functional. Chicanas are among those in dysfunctional relationships that have hurt both men and women, although often it is women in these relationships who become physical and psychological victims of abusive men.

It is ironic and sexist that women (the victims) endure blaming-the-victim theoretical models when some social scientists explain this phenomenon. They often do it to themselves, placing too much blame on themselves for making bad choices in men. For Chicanas what a woman does about this is a political act. An interesting insight into women who make bad choices emerges in Robin Norwood's *Women Who Love Too Much* (1985). Her fundamental premise is that some women become addicted to relationships. Their desire to love, their yearning, their actual loving, is a form of addiction. This is especially important to Chicanas who are reared with a high regard for children, marriage, and family. Many of these women get into dependent relationships, especially if they come from dysfunctional families and were traumatized in childhood. These women align themselves with men who are physically or emotionally unavailable or who continue to traumatize them.

A woman who loves too much thinks she can change her abusive man. Such a woman feels that if only she could make him happy, make him feel her love for him, if only he understood her positive desires for him, their relationship would be beautiful. Such a woman tries to make the relationship work even at an unusual cost to herself, but it cannot. There is no basis for a healthy relationship in this type of codependency.

In traumatizing women, the abusive male, with the support of other social forces, will get the female to believe it is her fault that he is not happy. In his dependent illness he blames her for his addiction to alcohol, drugs, sports, or work. His tactic is to mask the real problem. He isolates the woman by cutting her off from friends and family, while she feeds into this by giving up any support network on behalf of making her relationship work.

Why are these women this way? Norwood's contentions are limited to white Anglo women, but she does shed some light on the nature of women's social oppression by stating that women are socialized to nurture. They carry nurturing characteristics into relationships with men who expect to be nurtured. Chicano women are also socialized to be communal, to place their own needs in conjunction with or second to the needs of the group. In part, the trap is social, understood in how genders are socialized. For example, men become addicted externally to drugs, alcohol, sports, and work, but they become addicted impersonally. They generally do not become addicted to people. Women become addicted to people. Some men do become addicted to other people, but this is more frequently a feminine trait. Women respond with sympathy and understanding to individuals who hurt, and they sometimes seek men upon whom they can practice what they have been taught.

For Chicana feminists, not to remain in abusive relationships is a political act that helps to liberate women and men. To stop taking advantage of sexist privilege helps males further the liberation movement of Chicano people. Chicano men have nothing to fear except their own unknown liberation. Unfortunately, the words *feminist* and *feminism* are alienating too many men. To some men they mean either "bra-burning women's libbers" or "feminine-like." Contemporary men are repelled by both the stereotyped radical female and the pink, powdery softness of women dependent on their femininity for male economic support.

To avoid resistance, to sensitize men to Chicana feminists, we need to find an androgynous term for feminism. *Egalitarian* is a term that includes both men and women with feminist convictions, convictions once at the heart of Chicano culture. Perhaps the designation should be Spanish. *Compadre* and *comadre* denote a commitment to family, to people. Whatever the term, it should make clear that the person being labeled respects and supports equal rights for all human beings. Feminists and egalitarians need not only say this but live their lives by what they say.

CLOSING THE GAP BETWEEN THEORY AND PRACTICE

Some differences between men and women complement the life cycle, but artificial differences complicate it and produce unnecessary stresses and conflicts. Men, including Chicano men, have taken advantage of privileges falsely accorded them by virtue of their male gender. In the process they have negated their responsibility to community. Men have a responsibility toward making the life cycle less stressful. Yet some men do not assume or accept this responsibility. They let women bear this burden. Some women, including Chicanas, have assumed this responsibility for themselves as well as for their men.

Many people believe they need someone to take care of them. Perhaps this desire exists because the burden of caretaking in contemporary society is too heavy. Caretaking no longer means only bringing home the paycheck; for Chicanos it means guarding against racism, sexism, and class discrimination; it means earning an income, being sexually responsible, and taking part in childrearing. It means the teaching of morals, values, and ethics. It also means tending an emotional, physical, and spiritual life. Because of changes in society, Chicano men have inherited, or at least have to share in, some of the work women once did. Some women, however, feel there is little need for men to invest in "women's" activities. Thus they feel more power and control if men are not involved in their sphere. At the same time, some women do not want men adopting feminist consciousness because they themselves might as a result have to face the world of "men's" work. Equality is threatening to these women. The truth here, however, is that economics requires a woman to contribute in ways she once did not have to contribute.

Also threatening to some women is having to direct their own lives. The women who speak against feminism prefer to remain sheltered from economic and political realities and from social stress. They prefer to let men bear the brunt of such visible stresses, and in this preference they contribute to the manipulation of gender roles that result in male oppression that also oppresses women. For feminist Chicanas this is dangerous and inhumane.

Males must share the blame for not coming forth to discuss openly how sexism oppresses them. Thus far, La Chicana has been at the forefront of discussions about male oppression. The very nature of the socially defined male-gender role leads men to commit more successful suicides and become victimized by drug and alcohol addiction. Men have more ulcers and more heart attacks. They are more likely to be criminals, to commit violent acts, and to die violent deaths. They suffer more social alienation, fear of war, and lack of appropriate social skills. It is in their interest to seek and participate in open discussion about the oppression of the social expectations of the male gender.

Feminist Chicanas are aware of minority male oppression and are searching for a political position on this subject. They are aware that Chicanas have certain expectations of their men, pressuring them to provide the material comforts they see and believe Anglo men provide for Anglo women. Yet minority men are barred from achieving the means by which to obtain these comforts, even for themselves. Chicanas need to enter into different relationships with minority men, although men need to cooperate by not taking advantage of male privilege.

The majority of males in the United States have a sense of power. For Chicano men this sense is mostly false. The notion that they possess real power keeps them participating in an oppressive system. Their mythology or justification for participation is that at least as men they have more resources than women.

With change in the use of language and some simple changes in behavior, men and women would experience the end of internalized discriminatory behavior that poses contradictory and conflicting dichotomies, the oppressive nature of which is not always obvious. If men want to live longer, want to live in peace, want to rid their society of discrimination and lead a less stressful life, they will join the ranks of those who have become egalitarianist *compadres*, and they will support feminist and minority movements.

In reality, if gender roles were relaxed, most men would live less stressful lives with fewer suicides, less alcoholism, less drug addiction, and fewer ulcers. Fewer men would die of heart attacks at the age of forty-five or fifty, and going to war would be debatable because violence to settle differences would not be the sole alternative. Men would not make war, and women and children would not have to endure it.

FURTHERING THE PARADIGM SHIFT

Some families are clearly patriarchal. The division of labor in some requires women in the home to wield real, visible power; in others, the man presents a strong public presence but it is the woman who runs the show. This structure was disrupted by the U.S. war with Mexico and the signing of the Treaty of Guadalupe Hidalgo. From this period the Chicano emerged as a conquered person, having endured the physical and social disruption characterized by conquest. The result was a unique experience, deviant in that it is not the dominant experience. Like Native American culture, Chicano culture is also unique in that it has not been erased and yet it has not totally conformed to Anglo dimensions. Chicano attempts to restructure along patriarchal and matriarchal lines have failed. Matriarchy will not be tolerated by patriarchy, and patriarchy will not be tolerated by matriarchy. Therefore, the battle of the sexes ensues, and Chicanos are caught in the cross fire.

The paradigm shift demanded by women and by racial and ethnic minorities requires a new language or language structure, one that places women and minorities within the educational, economic, and political arenas. As Emma Pérez (1990a) noted at the 1990 NACS conference, men continue to talk to men in male language. They continue to want women to accept their dominance at the expense of female sanity. Chicanas refuse to comply, and, as related by Demetria Martinez (1990) at the same conference, they move to recognize that some of us are selected representatives of the colonized women who are showcased by the colonizer in order to better colonize or silence the uncolonized and those who are not yet fully colonized. Martinez advocates the reclaiming of language by women because they bear the brunt of infant mortality and poverty and this is their source of authority. She further contends that Chicano assimilation is an Anglo fallacy and that Chicano struggle means they have not succeeded. Both Martinez and Pérez use language that criticizes social penetration (or cultural blending), rape, and control. Both note that Chicano males and females are addicted to what destroys them. They mimic heterosexual, colonized models, and they do so to survive. Chicanas now demand a new way of looking at and living life.

They require conscious direction of culture, a move away from gender centricity. This consists of a primary challenge. Such a move will, for example, assist researchers in reanalyzing gangs as patriarchally identified groups (*vatos*). Considered from a new perspective, Chicano gang members are deviant only because they have identified patriarchally, have been dispossessed of identity, and have accepted patriarchal values. Male gangs do not provide a viable alternative to racism. In fact, they are groups that have very strongly internalized sexism and racism. In accepting the gang role they oppress themselves by perpetuating a limiting social system.

The same is true of the Chicana single-parent family. Rather than being identified as a healthy adaptation to oppression, the single-parent family is considered dysfunctional. Given their patriarchal perspective, dominant social scientists need to see the Chicana single-parent family as deviant in order for it to make sense. But the dominant society is wrong. Its vision is limited because it does not see the positive, the functional aspects of the female single-parent family. Indeed, it refuses to see such a family as healthy because its own patriarchal structure neither allows nor tolerates either functional or dysfunctional Chicano families. It hates Chicanos and Chicanas. Social scientists need a perverted view of women of color in order to justify their racist, sexist activities.

Resistance to alternative world views, or a shift in the paradigm, is made clear when lesbian women and homosexual men begin to talk about structural change. Neither colonized patriarchal nor colonized matriarchal Chicano structures allow or tolerate homosexuality and lesbianism. The existence of arguments against same-sex acts documents dominant colonized resistance to alternatives and to creative holistic thinking. The question "Is homosexuality normal and even healthy for some as a reaction against the rigidity of patriarchy and colonized matriarchy?" is never asked. In fact, it is surprising to discover that anyone can even think to ask the question. The surprise is enlightening, for what has been achieved is not only lateral and critical thinking but is holistic thinking. Only someone with a varied firsthand cultural experience, like a lesbian Chicana, could ever begin to think this way.

TO HEAL A NATION

Soon the world will celebrate the quincentenary of the Spanish discovery of the New World. The Americas did not need discovering, of course, for indigenous people lived there long before any European set foot on its soil or even knew there was land on this side of the world.

After five hundred years, racism is alive and well in the United States. Our country is hurting, and many are tired of seeing it suffer. It is time to discuss its healing.

Racism is a sickness. Racists internalize their own superiority, disdaining and degrading others. The racist's victims sometimes accept the disdain, or they grind their teeth in hate and even destroy themselves. Few minorities escape feeling they must constantly prove themselves. Some succeed, but others fail. The dynamics allow our nation to live a biased history, on the one hand, and a suppressed history, on the other. We live a lie, an unfulfilled, artificial lie, of justice and equality for all.

But how does a nation heal from the atrocities committed against itself? How does a huge group of people reach a consensus on how to live and how not to live, especially when in the past groups have been estranged from one another? How can a minority group forget and move beyond forgiveness when its members have agonized so much? When they have been victimized, demeaned, disgraced, humiliated, and so very badly crippled?

Chicanos grieve. They grieve as a people. They grieve as families and individual men, children, and women. They grieve as an entire culture. Although they want to heal, the first step for them, and for our country, is anger, blatant, expressed, or internalized anger: the anger of the 1960s. Uneven progress is being made on issues of oppression. Some Chicanos are stalemated in this angry phase. In this anger people slow themselves down. They ruin themselves, devastate others. Without guidance some have moved beyond anger to create alternative lifestyles. It is time to move beyond this grieving state, beyond the first-aid phase of putting Band-Aids on wounds in systems of education, politics, health care, criminal justice, and religion.

It is time to continue the healing process by taking the next steps: acceptance of the reality, acknowledgment, and acceptance of the pain. It is time, once again, to grow from what we know. It is for some a time to be assertive in pushing the United States into a state of health by nudging it into a more creative and holistic stage.

Perhaps the nation will have to hurt when it faces up to the suffering and devastation its dominant society has caused others. Perhaps it is time descendants of the conquistadors and the indigenous Indians confront the fact that their European ancestors raped, killed, and enslaved hordes of Indians also. Perhaps blacks need to accept that they have become more like the white man than they would like to admit, and women must face the fact that some of them have internalized a male-dominated value system.

Perhaps some of us will have to be upset when noting that, right or wrong, good or bad, U.S. history is our history. We have taught it. We have sanctioned it. We have lived it. Perhaps we will be embarrassed and even more angry recognizing that we have inherited something we did not ourselves fully create, and that we have not done much about it. Perhaps we will be ashamed to have profited from class discrimination, racism, and sexism. Perhaps we will hesitate to change that which brings us comfort.

Even though these are old ways, we must work through them in order to heal, for these are the ways that stifle creativity and that no longer serve to keep our nation a leader. In fact, we need to rethink leadership. The United States can no longer be at the front, on top, alone. It has to share international leadership. Those who resist are grounded in antiquated ways, in wishful thinking, denying that the world has changed, that minorities are the majority, and that our nation has been resistant to change. Dominant Americans have to give up their sole claim to privilege, and minority Americans have to accept their ownership.

Of course, there will be those who do not like the latest developments in their democracy. No matter. This nation must do what is right for itself. In its self-interest, it must adopt new ways of thinking, new ways of behaving. It must engage in values clarification. It must face the great contradiction that maintains that there is freedom and justice for all but demonstrates it is only for those who can afford it. Further, democracy as an ideal must be consistent with its practice. Democracy means that most Americans get to participate, not just react to what a few have outlined for us. It means that information, and access to information, is a fundamental human right. To deny information is to violate the truths that some consider to be self-evident.

It is a new world, in which our culture lags behind technology. Old attitudes pit Americans against Japanese, Anglos against Hispanics, and keep cultures and civilizations from advancing. Advance they will, however, whether we like it or not. Those who change with the times help shape the times. Those who linger behind stay behind.

REFERENCES

Blea, Irene I. 1988. *Toward a Chicano Social Science*. New York: Praeger. 144-46.

______. 1990. *Bessemer: A Sociological Perspective of a Chicano Barrio*. New York: AMS Press.

Durkheim, Emile. 1915. *The Elementary Forms of the Religious Life*. London: George Allen and Unwin.

Fannon, Franz. 1963. *The Wretched of the Earth.* New York: Grove Press.

Garcia Rivas, Heriberto. 1988. *Cocina Pre-Hispanica Mexicana.* Mexico, D.F.: Colección Panorama.

Isasi-Díaz, Ada María, and Yolanda Tarango. 1988. *Hispanic Women: Prophetic Voice in the Church.* San Francisco: Harper & Row. 1-10.

Lizarraga, Sylvia S. 1988. "Hacia una Teoria para la Liberación de la Mujer." In Juan R. Garcia, Julia Curry Rodriguez, and Clara Lomas, eds., *In Times of Challenge: Chicanos and Chicanas in American Society.* Texas: University of Houston Press, Mexican-American Studies Program, Monograph Series No. 6. 25-31.

Martinez, Demetria. 1990. Presentation made during the Chicana Plenary at the 1990 National Association for Chicano Studies Conference, Albuquerque, New Mexico.

Memmi, Albert. 1965. *The Colonizer and the Colonized.* Boston: Beacon Press.

Mosqueda, Lawrence. 1986. *Chicanos, Catholicism and Political Ideology*. New York: University of America Press. 154-55.

Norwood, Robin. 1985. *Women Who Love Too Much.* New York: Simon and Schuster.

Pérez, Emma. 1990a. "Sexuality and Discourse: Unmaking and Making Latina Space and Language." Unpublished paper presented at the 1990 National Association for Chicano Studies Conference, Albuquerque, New Mexico.

______. 1990b. "Sexuality and Discourse from the Margin: A Chicana Lesbian Historical Materialist Perspective." Unpublished paper presented at the 1990 National Association for Chicano Studies Conference, Albuquerque, New Mexico.

Trujillo, Carla, ed. 1991. *Chicana Lesbians: The Girls Our Mothers Warned Us About.* Berkeley: Third Woman Press.

Selected Bibliography

Acuna, Rodolfo. 1981. *Occupied America: A History of Chicanos*, 3rd ed. New York: Harper & Row.

Almaguer, Tomás. 1974. "Historical Notes on Chicano Oppression: The Dialectics of Racial and Class Domination in North America." *Aztlán: Chicano Journal of the Social Sciences and the Arts*, 5 (Spring-Fall): 27-56.

Aragon, Janie Louise. 1976. "The People of Santa Fe in the 1790's." *Aztlán: Journal of International Chicano Studies*, Vol. 7, No. 3.

Baca-Zinn, Maxine. 1975a. "Political Familism: Toward Sex Role Equality in Chicano Families." *Aztlán: Chicano Journal of the Social Sciences and the Arts*, 6 (Spring): 13-26.

______. 1975b. "Chicanas: Power and Control in the Domestic Sphere." *De Colores*, Vol. 1, No. 3.

Baca-Zinn, Maxine, Lynn Cannon, Elizabeth Higgenbotham, and Bonnie Thorton Dill. 1986. "The Costs of Exclusionary Practices in Women's Studies." *Signs: Journal of Women in Culture and Society*, Vol. 2, No. 21.

Barrera, Mario. 1979. *Race and Class in the Southwest*. South Bend, Ind.: University of Notre Dame Press.

______. 1988. *Beyond Aztlan: Ethnic Autonomy in Comparative Perspective*. New York: Praeger.

Blea, Irene. 1990. *Bessemer: A Sociological Perspective of a Chicano Barrio*. New York: AMS Press.

______. 1988. *Toward a Chicano Social Science*. New York: Praeger.

______. 1988. *"La Entriega de Novios:* The Cultural Practice of Being Given and Taken in Marriage." Unpublished manuscript, paper presented at Hispanic Cultures of the Americas Conference, Barcelona, Spain.

Camacho de Schmidt, Aurora. 1988. "Violence and a Non-Violent Movement." *Hispanic Link Weekly Report*, Vol. 6, No. 7 (November 7): 4.

Cantu, Norma. 1986. "Women, Then and Now: An Analysis of the Adelita Image Versus the Chicana as Political Writer and Philosopher." In Theresa Cordova et al, eds., *Chicana Voices: Intersections of Class, Race and Gender*. Austin: University of Texas Press.

Cordova, Teresa, Norma Cantu, Gilberto Cardenas, Juan Garcia, and Christine M. Sierra, eds. 1986. *Chicana Voices: Intersections of Class, Race and Gender*. Austin: University of Texas Press.

Cotera, Martha. 1976. *Diosa y Hembra*. Austin: Information Systems Development.

Davila, Bill. 1988. "Back to the Future." *Hispanic: The Magazine of the Contemporary Hispanic*. (July): 13.

De la Garza, R., and R. Brischetto. 1983. "The Mexican-American Electorate: Information Sources and Policy Orientations." Occasional Paper No. 2, San Antonio, Texas, Southwest Voter Registration Education Project and the Hispanic Population Studies Program of the Center for Mexican-American Studies. Austin: University of Texas.

Díaz del Castillo, Bernal. 1963. *The Conquest of New Spain*. Trans. J. M. Cohen. New York: Penguin Books.

Durkheim, Emile. 1915. *The Elementary Forms of the Religious Life*. London: George Allen and Unwin.

Elsasser, Nan, Kyle MacKenzie, and Yvonne Tixier y Vigil. 1980. *Las Mujeres: Conversations from a Hispanic Community*. New York: Feminist Press.

Fannon, Frantz. 1963. *The Wretched of the Earth*. New York: Grove Press.

Figueroa Torres, J. Jesús. 1975. In B. Costa-Amic, ed., *Doña Marina: Una India Ejemplar*. Mexico, D.F.: B. Costa-Amic.

Firestone, Shulamith. 1972. *The Dialectic of Sex*. New York: Bantam Books.

Garcia, Alma M. 1986. "Studying Chicanas: Bringing Women into the Frame of Chicano Studies." In Theresa Cordova et al., eds. *Chicana Voices: Intersections of Class, Race, and Gender*. Austin: CMAS Publications, University of Texas Press.

Garcia, Christina. 1988. "Shake Your Body." In "Magnifico! Hispanic Culture Breaks Out of the Barrio." *Time*, Vol. 132 (July 11): 50-52.

Garcia, John. 1983. "Chicano Political Development: Examining Participation in the Decade of Hispanics." National Chicano Council of Higher Education, *La Red/The Network*, No. 72 (September).

Garcia, John, Julia Curry Rodriguez, and Clara Lomas, eds. 1988. *Times of Challenge: Chicanos and Chicanas in American Society*. Houston: University of Houston Press, Mexican American Studies Program, Monograph Series No. 6.

Gomez Tagle, Silvia, Adrian Garcia Valdes, and Lourdes Grobet. 1985. *National Museum of Anthropology*. Trans. Joan Ingram-Eiser. Mexico, D.F.: Distribución Cultural Especializada.

Griswold del Castillo, Richard. 1988. "The Chicano Movement and the Treaty of Guadelupe Hidalgo." In Juan R. Garcia, Julia Curry Rodriguez, and Clara Lomas, eds. *Times of Challenge: Chicanos and Chicanas in American Society*. Houston: University of Houston Press, Mexican-American Studies Program, Monograph Series No. 6.

______. 1984. *La Familia: Chicano Families in the Urban Southwest: 1848 to the Present*. South Bend, Ind.: University of Notre Dame Press.

Hernandez Tovar, Inés. 1975. "Para Teresa." In *An Anthology of Chicano Literature*. Austin: Chicano Studies Center.

Hispania. 1989. "Hispana Smokers Increase While Men Light Up Less," Vol. 3, No. 4: 1.

Hispanic Link Weekly Report. 1989. Vol. 7, No. 7 (February 20): 2.

Hurtado, Aida. 1987. "Midwife Practices in Hidalgo County, Texas." *Trabajos Monográficos: Studies in Chicana/Latina Research*, Vol. 3, No. 1: 1-30.

Isasi-Díaz. Ada María, and Yolanda Tarango. 1988. *Hispanic Women: Prophetic Voice in the Church*. San Francisco: Harper & Row.

Kiev, Aria. 1968. *Curanderismo, Mexican American Folk Psychiatry*. New York: Free Press.

Lacayo, Richard. 1988. "A Surging New Spirit." In "Magnífico! Hispanic Culture Breaks Out of the Barrio." *Time*, Vol. 132 (July 11): 46-49. This article was reported by Scott Brown, Christina Garcia, and Edward M. Gomez.

Lopez-Garza, Marta C. 1986. "Toward a Reconceptualization of Women's Economic Activities: The Informal Sector in Urban Mexico." In Theresa Cordova *et al.*, eds., *Chicana Voices: Intersections of Class, Race, and Gender*. Austin: CMAS Publications, University of Texas Press.

Martinez, Demetria. 1990. "In Whose Interest: Reclaiming the Language of National Security." Unpublished paper presented at the 1990 National Association for Chicano Studies Conference, Albuquerque, New Mexico.

McWilliams, Carey. 1968. *North of Mexico: The Spanish Speaking People of the United States*. New York: Greenwood Press.

Mejias-Renta, 1989. "The Coming Home of Carmen Zapata," *Vista*, March 12.

Melville, Margaritta B. 1980. *Twice a Minority: Mexican-American Women*. St. Louis, Mo.: Mosby Press.

Memmi, Albert. 1965. *The Colonizer and the Colonized*. Boston: Beacon Press.

Mirande, Alfredo, and Evangelina Enriquez. 1979. *La Chicana*. Chicago: University of Chicago Press.

______. 1987. *Gringo Justice*. South Bend, Ind.: University of Notre Dame Press.

Mosqueda, Lawrence. 1986. *Chicanos, Catholicism and Political Ideology*. New York: University of America Press.

Nicholson, Irene. 1968. *A Guide to Mexican Poetry: Ancient and Modern*. Mexico, D.F.: Editorial Minutiae Mexicana.

Norwood, Robin. 1985. *Women Who Love Too Much*. New York: Simon and Schuster.

Olivera, Mercedes. 1989. "The Latina's Juggling Act." *Vista: Focus on Hispanic Americans*, Vol. 4, No. 15 (December): 15.

Orozco, Cynthia. 1986. "Sexism in Chicano Studies and in the Community." In Theresa Cordova et al., eds., *Chicana Voices: Intersections of Class, Race, and Gender*. Austin: CMAS Publications, University of Texas Press.

Pena, Devon. 1986. "Between the Lines: A New Perspective on the Industrial Sociology of Women Workers in Transnational Labor Processes." In Theresa Cordova et al., eds., *Chicana Voices: Intersections of Class, Race, and Gender*. Austin: CMAS Publications, University of Texas Press.

Perez, Emma. 1990a. "Sexuality and Discourse: Unmaking and Making Latina Space and Language." Unpublished paper presented at the 1990 National Association for Chicano Studies Conference, Albuquerque, New Mexico.

______. 1990b. "Sexuality and Discourse from the Margin: A Chicana Lesbian Historical Materialist Perspective." Unpublished paper presented at the 1990 National Association for Chicano Studies Conference, Albuquerque, New Mexico.

______. 1991. "Sexuality and Discourse: Notes from a Chicana Survivor." In Carla Trujillo, ed., *Chicana Lesbians: The Girls Our Mothers Warned Us About.* Berkeley: Third Woman Press.

Pesquera, Beatriz M., and Denise Segura. 1989. Paper presented at the Western Social Science Association Annual Conference, Albuquerque, New Mexico. Also appeared as a short synopsis in the 1988 MALCS newsletter.

(La) Raza Unida Archives. Austin: University of Texas, Benson Latin-American Col-lection.

Rocky Mountain News. 1982. "Gene Flaw Is Tracked to 1700s." *Rocky Mountain News* (August 31): 13.

Ryan, William. 1971. *Blaming the Victim*. New York: Vintage Books.

Saiz, Flor. 1973. *La Chicana.* Denver: La Chicana Publications.

Segura, Denise A. 1986. "Chicanas and Triple Oppression in the Labor Force." In Theresa Cordova et al., eds. *Chicana Voices: Intersections of Class, Race, and Gender*. Austin: CMAS Publications, University of Texas Press.

Sierra, Christine Marie. 1988. "Chicano Politics after 1984." In Juan R. Garcia, Julia Curry Rodriguez, and Clara Lomas, eds., *Times of Challenge: Chicanos and Chicanas in American Society*. Texas: University of Houston Press, Mexican-American Studies Program, Monograph Series No. 6.

______. 1986. "Chicano Politics After 1984." In Theresa Cordova et al., eds., *Chicana Voices: Intersections of Class, Race, and Gender.* Austin: CMAS Publications, University of Texas Press, pp. 5-7.

Soto, Shirlene. 1990. *Emergence of the Modern Mexican Woman: Her Participation in Revolution and Struggle for Equality 1910-1940.* Denver, Colo: Arden Press.

Swadesh, Frances Leon. 1974. *Los Primeros Pobladores*. South Bend, Ind.: University of Notre Dame Press.

Torres, J. Jesús Figueroa. 1975. In B. Costa-Amic, ed., *Doña Marina: Una India Ejemplar.* Mexico City: B. Costa-Amic.

Trotter, Robert T., II, and Juan Antonio Chavira. 1981. *Curanderismo: Mexican-American Health and Religion.* Athens, Ga.: University of Georgia Press.

Trujillo, Carla, ed. 1991. *Chicana Lesbians: The Girls Our Mothers Warned Us About.* Berkeley: Third Woman Press.

U.S. Department of Commerce, Bureau of Census. 1987. *The Statistical Abstract of the United States,* 108th ed. Washington, D.C.: GPO.

Venya, Angelina F. 1986. "Women in Early New Mexico: A Preliminary View." In Theresa Cordova et al., eds., *Chicana Voices: Intersections of Class, Race, and Gender.* Austin: CMAS Publications, University of Texas Press.

______. 1985. "Una Vista al Pasado: La Mujer en Nuevo Mexico 1744-1767." *Trabajos Monográficos: Studies in Chicana/Latina Research,* Vol. 1, No. 1.

Ybarra, Leonarda. 1977. "Conjugal Role Relationships in the Chicano Family." Ph.D. dissertation, University of California, Berkeley.

______. 1982. "When Wives Work: The Impact on the Chicano Family." *Journal of Marriage and the Family,* 44 (February): 169-78.

______. 1982. "Marital Decision-Making and the Role of Machismo in the Chicano Family." *De Colores,* Vol. 6, Nos. 1 & 2: 32-47.

Index

ABOUT THE AUTHOR

IRENE I. BLEA is Director of Hispanic Student Affairs at the University of New Mexico. She received her Ph.D. in sociology from the University of Colorado. She has taught race and gender relations courses for fifteen years and has been instrumental in the development of Chicano studies. She is the national chair of the Chicana Caucus of the National Association of Chicano Studies. Author of *Toward a Chicano Social Science* (Praeger, 1988) and *Bessemer: A Sociological Perspective of a Chicano Barrio* (1988), she has also published numerous articles, poetry, and a play, and is working on a historical novel.

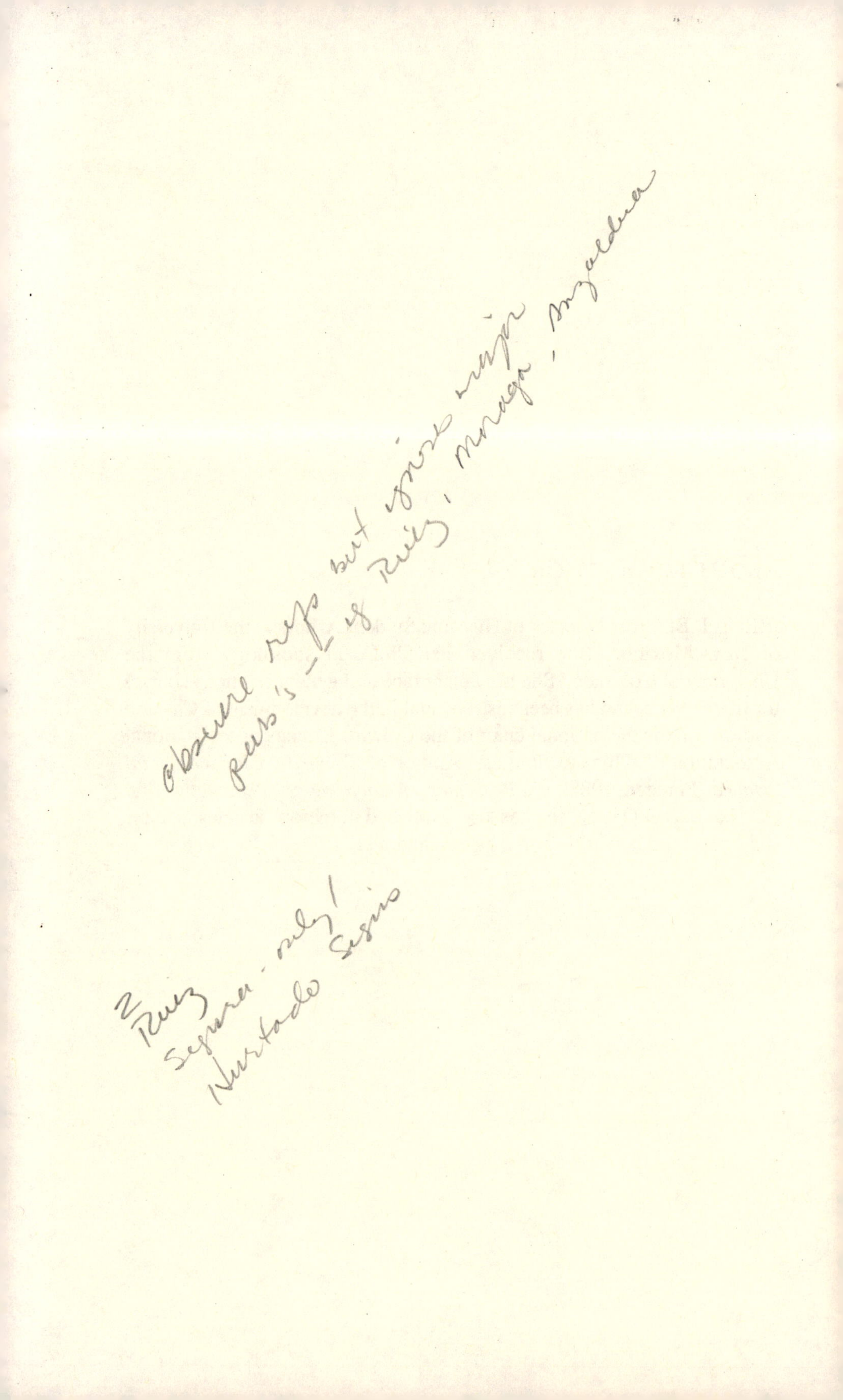